Praise for *The In-Between*

"*The In-Between* is a tribute to resilience in the face of adversity. Filled with compassion and tenderness, this memoir in verse will resonate with anyone who has ever felt stuck in between parents, in between homes, or in between childhood and adulthood."

—MEGAN E. FREEMAN, award-winning poet
and author of *Alone*

"Van Heidrich masterfully describes her childhood emotions as well her mother's confusing choices and mental health struggles with compassion and nuance. Stellar writing, perfect pacing, and a sophisticated treatment of universal themes make this a must-read."

—*Kirkus Reviews*, starred review

"Van Heidrich's work is ideal for readers who enjoy real-world stories that read like fiction and don't shy away from struggle."

—*Booklist*

"Van Heidrich skillfully depicts the complexities of housing insecurity, financial precarity, and adolescent growing pains via lyrical text in this unflinching yet hopeful read."

—*Publishers Weekly*

"Van Heidrich . . . reaches an emotional inflection point that she shares with readers."

—*Horn Book*

THE In-Between

by Katie Van Heidrich

aladdin
NEW YORK   LONDON   TORONTO   SYDNEY   NEW DELHI

Certain names and other characteristics have been changed.

ALADDIN

An imprint of Simon & Schuster Children's Publishing Division

1230 Avenue of the Americas, New York, New York 10020

First Aladdin paperback edition January 2024

Text copyright © 2023 by Katie Wingate

Cover illustrations copyright © 2024 by Ana Latese

Also available in an Aladdin hardcover edition.

All rights reserved, including the right of reproduction in whole or in part in any form.

ALADDIN and related logo are registered trademarks of Simon & Schuster, LLC.

Simon & Schuster: Celebrating 100 Years of Publishing in 1924

For information about special discounts for bulk purchases, please contact Simon & Schuster Special Sales at 1-866-506-1949 or business@simonandschuster.com.

The Simon & Schuster Speakers Bureau can bring authors to your live event. For more information or to book an event contact the Simon & Schuster Speakers Bureau at 1-866-248-3049 or visit our website at www.simonspeakers.com.

Cover designed by Karin Paprocki

Interior designed by Mike Rosamilia

The text of this book was set in Baskerville.

Manufactured in the United States of America 1223 OFF

2 4 6 8 10 9 7 5 3 1

Library of Congress Control Number 2022946897

ISBN 9781665920124 (hc)

ISBN 9781665920131 (pbk)

ISBN 9781665920148 (ebook)

To my sonshines, Brandon and Nasir,
and my brilliant niece, Taylor.

And to all the young people currently in between
where they want to be and where they are—
keep going. It gets better.

Things Fall Apart

With each move,
I sort and pack,
pack and sort.

Everything has its place,
its compartment,
books and
pictures and
feelings, too
and
with each move,
there are fewer boxes to carry.

I'm only thirteen
but I've done a lot of living and moving,
finding that all things
eventually fall apart,
in time,
no matter how well packed.

I Don't Need a Cosigner

A moment ago, we'd just gotten in
from the eight-and-a-half-hour drive
back home to Atlanta from East St. Louis.

We'd only been gone for a few days,
to attend Grandpa Puckett's funeral,
who wasn't really blood but who stepped up anyway,
who watched over and cared for our family anyway,
when there wasn't really anyone else to be Grandpa.

And as if visiting Mom's hometown wasn't disaster enough,
as if visiting a city we only seem to visit when there's
    mourning to be done
wasn't tragedy enough,
the ride back was grueling—
thick, stifling air growing more stale by the hour
as we bickered over the radio,
over where we'd stop for food,
over whose turn it was
to sit in the front seat.

Eight and a half hours of
You've got one more time, Haley

and *Watch your mouth, Josh*
and *I don't need a cosigner, Katie* (to me)
and *I will pull this car over right here, right NOW* to all three of us
until finally,
by the grace of God Almighty,
we turned off Roswell Road
and into the parking lot of our apartment complex,
tires crunching gravel,
coming to a full stop in front of our building,
our apartment windows
eerily dark.

As we tumbled out of the Mountaineer,
which seems to be on its last leg,
to stretch our arms and legs,
to gather fast-food wrappers and
empty soda cups in gas station plastic bags,
to grab our bags from the trunk and
make our way upstairs and to our door,
an unexplainable pit appeared in my stomach
and continued to grow as we climbed the stairs.

And though I couldn't have possibly known it then,
I somehow felt that we were walking into
a much bigger disaster than anything
we'd already managed to survive.

Broken Promises

What's that smell?
Mom, why won't the lights turn on?
Why is it so cold?

Our ping-pong questions go unanswered
as Mom runs to open Claire's crate,
as Mom runs to comfort the pleading whimpers and cries
    that fill the air,
air that is also thick with the uncompromising smell of waste.
We look closer and see that the landlord did *not* in fact
let her out or feed her
as promised,
work something out to keep the lights or heat on,
as promised,
which means we also can probably
kiss his promise to give Mom more time with the rent
goodbye.

Mom! They're all DEAD! Josh scream-cries from his room.

Four days into 2003
and everything is already
a disaster.

Volcanoes

My siblings and I
are three volcanoes,
though we are not the same
in how we erupt,
let alone how often.

Josh is mostly dormant,
quiet and reserved,
until he's not,
quiet and to himself,
until he's not.

He can be an enigma,
a total and complete mystery,
off and away
in the corners of his mind,
off and away
in the corners of the universe
he's built for himself
and himself alone,
complete with Pokémon cards
we can't touch and
episodes of *Dragon Ball Z*

we are warned not to change and
round after round after round after round
of *Grand Theft Auto*.

He has a certain nonchalance
about homework that contrasts
with my need to be most pleasing
and bring home all As,
but a penchant for building things
out of everyday household items
and creating culinary masterpieces
out of everyday pantry items,
what little remains in between paydays,
like ramen,
which, to me,
shows how resourceful
and practical he is.

Haley, on the other hand,
is an active volcano,
prone to spewing hot lava
and burning everything in her path
because she can.

She holds back nothing,
freely speaking her mind

without fear or consequence,

despite frequent consequences

for her jokes and commentary,

which often go unappreciated.

And though I don't always agree with her,

there are times

she says what I can't

and does what I won't,

out of fear of making Mom mad,

or worse,

sad.

Her words are highly respected daggers,

so long as they're not aiming at you.

She's quick to say

I need to grow thicker skin

and I'm quick to ask

why she insists on making

already-tense situations tenser

but the comedian in her

is more likely to laugh and

spin on her heels,

leaving you feeling

mindless and

spineless,

too.

As for me,

I've been dormant so long

I might as well be

an extinct volcano.

I'm known for going along

to get along,

capable of making sense

of whatever Mom decides she needs to do,

no matter how suddenly

or sharply her decisions might change

from what was previously decided and promised,

which irritates my siblings but gains me

favor with Mom,

which I prefer.

Fish Guts and Glass

In my brother's room,

his prized fish float

upside down—

more evidence of the landlord's

broken promises—

their bloated bellies

one pin's prick away

from popping and exploding.

Josh,

who is also always

one pin's prick away from popping and exploding,

storms out of the room.

Haley and I stare in disbelief

until we rejoin him in the front,

finding him sitting on the living room floor,

hands cupping his shaking forehead,

single tears dotting the hardwood.

Mom is here too, now,

crossing the room back and forth,

s l o w l y at first,

but soon quickening her pace,

silent but furious,

silent but fuming,

silent but clearly plotting.

Suddenly, and without warning,

she bounds two steps at a time

back to Josh's room and moments later,

darts back across the living room

with Wonder Woman speed,

hauling the fish tank with both hands

with Wonder Woman strength,

somehow managing not to spill a drop.

Get the door!

she yells to no one in particular

and since Haley is now

tasked with holding Claire

to keep her from smearing

poop all over the house,

and Josh is still dotting the floor

with his despair,

I jump to swing open the door.

I don't know what Mom plans to do on the other side of that
door,

which is typical,

but I'm thinking it is in my very best interest to help where I can, right now,

which is also typical.

Mom? I ask nervously.

She doesn't answer or

bother looking my way.

Instead, she holds the fish tank

high above her head,

careful not to drip

any of the rancid water

over herself and

without announcement or explanation,

sends the entire tank crashing

down

     down

          down

below,

exploding right onto

our landlord's doorstep downstairs.

Haley curses under her breath.

Mom, still in her trance,

doesn't even notice.

We know better than to say another word

or ask another question,

let alone

rush out to see what's happening.

I imagine the mix of

glass and putrid water,

rock and dead fish

seeping into the already-repugnant

dark carpet floor below.

I am equally impressed and scared out of my mind—

I can't help but respect

Mom's rage, which, in this moment,

demands to know,

How dare you mess with my children?

Without announcement or explanation,

Mom calmly spins on her heels

and returns back inside,

slamming the door and dead-bolting it too,

before squatting in front of us all,

her hands massaging her temples in small circles,

her brows rising and falling with the rotating of her fingers.

Because she is silent,

we are silent too,

minus the sound of Claire's tail

now happily wagging as if to say,
Welcome home, family.
After what seems like a very long time,
Mom stands and
walks the short steps to the kitchen.
She rummages through drawers and
then returns with handfuls of candles,
which she saves for times like these.

We'll need these tonight,
she says
as she tosses a few our way.
There are instructions, then,
to get Claire and ourselves cleaned up
and ready for bed,
with warnings of
a very long day ahead of us
tomorrow.

We all know what that means.

Whereas before it was a matter of *if* we were moving,
now the matter of *when* has been decided, too,
and much sooner than we expected, at that.

But thank God for Mom's intuition—

she bought extra trash bags and boxes before we left for the
   funeral—

and thank God for ours—

we kept some of the boxes we used from the move last year,

or was it the move before that?

I really can't be sure.

Without a word,

or any idea of whether hell or the police,

or a combination of both,

are going to show up tonight,

we move out immediately,

as if following military orders from a general who,

despite her four-foot-eleven frame,

commands both fear and respect, who,

despite her chaos,

remains our biggest advocate.

And while I'm hoping

that this is the very worst

of the disaster I felt brewing

as we initially climbed the stairs

to our apartment just ten minutes ago—

what now feels like a lifetime ago—

the pit in my stomach continues to expand,

telling me

that we're just

getting started.

It's Morning Time

which means
it's moving time,
which means
we better get going because
Mom's already been up for hours,
as evidenced by the smell of coffee and cigarettes,
her breakfast of champions.

It's morning time
which means
its moving time
which means
we better get going because
if we don't move fast enough,
decisions will be made for us,
as they have been done
so many times before,
leaving us with little,
if anything,
to decide for ourselves.

Where Are We Going?

We sluggishly start in our bedrooms with garbage bags—
Josh in his
and Haley and I
in the room we share—
tossing the obvious and not-so-obvious trash,
before Mom comes with the instructions to
Pack a suitcase, your school stuff, and put the rest in these boxes.
And one more thing, she says as she peers back into our room.
Keep the boxes light.

Where are we going?
   I thought we were supposed to . . .
        But, Mom! You said we'd have the chance to . . .

Haley and I word-vomit questions that will go unanswered
   for now,
since Mom is already down the hall and
in the bathroom we all share,
tossing half-empty bottles of
soaps and shampoo into the trash.

We continue the process of
trashing and sorting,

sorting and trashing,

reminding each other to

Keep the boxes light

when we notice the other is

clinging too tightly to things that should definitely be thrown

out,

like a B2K poster of mine

that's ripped at the edge

and Haley's treasured copy of *Justified*

that today

is just a case,

because the CD has long since disappeared.

Mom said keep it light, Haley,

I say to my sister as I notice her

stuffing bags with things

I don't think are necessary.

I say mind your business, Katie,

she replies,

and before I can snap back that

minding my siblings

has always been my business

as the oldest and most responsible child,

a still-solemn,

still-devastated,

still-grumbling Josh
stops at our doorway,
having pulled two large bags behind him.

Stop fighting and keep moving,
he says to us both.
Uncle Ronnie and Uncle Donny
will be here soon and
we don't have time to waste.

Haley and I exchange confused looks,
momentarily on the same page,
not realizing we were on *that* tight of a schedule and,
after shrugging,
get back to work.

I head to the living room and
snatch books from Mom's overflowing,
still-unpacked shelves,
to add to my already-growing collection
of books I've snatched from Mom's overflowing shelves,
figuring a good book
or three
will suit me well,
wherever we land.

I devour the books on Mama's shelves,

books like *Kindred* and

The Joy Luck Club and

The Women of Brewster Place and

any and everything by John Grisham,

though *The Testament* and *A Time to Kill*

and *The Runaway Jury* are among my favorites.

I like high stakes and history,

tragedy and perspective,

but what I like most,

what I take pride in most,

is simply reading what she reads,

even if I can't understand it all

(like when I tried to read *Beloved*),

even if I have to read with a dictionary by my side,

each completed book

a badge I proudly wear.

I swipe *A Painted House* and

I Know Why the Caged Bird Sings,

titles I've been meaning to get to.

Back in our room,

I set aside the thick

black CD case I carry everywhere,

carefully curated with my favorite artists—

artists like
Luther and Lauryn and Alicia and Donny
(what my friends call "sappy love songs")—
my Sony Walkman and headphones,
and the spiral notebook I've been
recently using to capture
disappointments and despairs,
feelings and hopes and
inspiring quotes, too.

I take a moment to jot down the date with the words:
MOVING AGAIN.
I underline the word *AGAIN* three times for emphasis
before stuffing the journal in my backpack for safekeeping.

Looks like I'll have plenty
to capture today
and in the days ahead.

As I continue the process
of combing through more books,
picture frames that capture happier, more stable times,
awards and report cards,
considering what to box and what to
keep for wherever it is in the world
that we're going,

I can't help but think
that we've done this too
many times before,
almost too many times before,
making us experts—
at moving, that is.

You Only Have Room for One

After all,
we've moved dozens of times before
and though each move has been different,
I've generally been able to put each move
into two distinct categories:
the slow moves and the fast moves.

Slow moves are the moves you see coming.

These are the moves that give you time—
time to carefully review each of your most beloved treasures,
time for proper goodbyes and
promises to stay in touch with friends you only recently
    made,
time for happy, mad dashes through freshly painted rooms
    with claims of,
Hey! We got here first from me and Haley or
You're out of your mind, this one is mine! from Josh.

Time to imagine
how you'll rearrange your books
and your stories
and maybe even yourself.

Years ago, I decided I wanted to be called Kitty
for the entirety of our nine-month stay in sunny Boca Raton.
When we landed in foggy San Francisco the following
    August
to follow a new fancy public relations job opportunity for
    Mom,
I transformed into Kathy.

Mom has always tried to make us feel better
when we've packed up in the middle of the year
and gone somewhere far.

Though they're difficult in their own ways,
I know all about these kinds of moves.
And after the adjusting period,
after the well-rehearsed school introductions
and attempts to explain to potential new friends
why you move so much—
offering things like
She got another job or
She lost another job, but I swear it's not her fault!—
I can confidently say that I like these moves best.

Other moves, however, have been lightning-fast—
    Quick! Which stuffed animal?

Big Bear or Eleanor? I remember asking
during one particularly quick move.

You only have room for one! Mom shouted
as she frantically ran a tape gun across a box
that held all our family pictures.
As she said this, she held a thick uncapped Sharpie
clenched between her teeth,
ready to label contents and mark boxes important.
And so, at her direction, I sent Big Bear soaring
into the one box of treasures we were allowed that move.
I squeezed Eleanor tightly on that evening flight
as Mom promised again and again
that Big Bear would be waiting for me
when we landed.

Later that night,
we sat stranded
at the airport's curbside pickup.
We waited anxiously for the businessman
who promised Mom relocation
and a new beginning,
waited anxiously for the businessman
who never came
until all three of us kids

were nodding in and out of sleep,
struggling to stay awake.

And as the hours continued to pass,
I knew in my heart
that Big Bear was lost forever
and so were our pictures,
our furniture—
any and everything
we had managed to gather
before that fateful night.

And even though
Mom wouldn't say it yet,
even though she couldn't
bring herself to say it quite yet,
her eyes told it all:
that sometimes,
even boxes marked important get lost.

I know these kinds of moves well too.

These are the moves
that force you to start over
when starting *completely* over
wasn't part of the plan.

These are the moves
that leave you sobbing
in new bedrooms full of *nothing*,
the ones that leave you
scanning and
staring down
what you managed to save,
wondering
if you made
the right
choice.

After all,
Big Bear was a gift from your father,
a most prized possession
you had since kindergarten,
while Eleanor came from your mother,
and what does this say of you?

What does this say
about what you chose to save
and what you allowed to be lost?

Over time, over long-distance phone calls,
your father will tell you *nothing*.
While over dinner,

your mother will say with deep sadness,
Oh, Katie.

But when you're nine,
these are the kinds of questions
that keep you up at night,
the kinds of questions
that follow long prayers to God
and make you wonder:
How much more will I lose?

It should go without saying
that I like these kinds of moves
least.

Roses and Thorns

Four years and a half-dozen moves
after we lost everything,
we landed in this dump,
this dump called Rose Hill,
which is the dumbest name
I've ever heard
for what is clearly
the most raggedy apartment complex
on earth.

When we first moved in,
Mom flashed a weak smile
and said something about
roses coming with thorns,
but silly her,
there never was and never has been
a garden here,
let alone roses.

There never was and never has been anything
but unkempt grass
and ragged concrete lots,
halls that reek of wet socks,

walls and floors that house

tiny, unwanted guests

that pitter-patter in the dark,

and,

when we moved in,

walls that sported old, peeling paint.

Despite the apparent hopelessness,

Mom used extra powers

to make inside our paradise.

Abracadabra!

Dingy kitchen walls

bloomed firehouse red.

Alakazam!

Rusty outlets

sparkled and glowed with the new gold covers,

discovered at Home Depot

for just a few dollars.

Mom hung new curtains

and framed portraits of

Dr. King speaking to

large groups of people and

Willie Mays slamming

wood against cowhide

to crowds of adoring fans,

making this dump
as close to a home
as we could recognize,
as best she could manage.

Mom worked magic
on the thorns of Rose Hill,
but not too much—
after all,
it's as if she already knew then
that we'd soon move again

and look at us this Saturday morning—
moving,
again.

It's Mourning Time

because
it's moving time
and this move,
I can already tell,
is going to be the fastest
of them all.

No Space for Us Now

That's the last of it,
Uncle Donny says to Mom,
as he and Uncle Ronnie
pull the back of the U-Haul truck closed.

It's dark now and we're out 20 East
at a U-Haul storage facility off Candler Road.
With no place to go,
we're storing the parts of our lives
that can't easily be carried,
things like furniture and bicycles and family pictures
that I pray we don't lose again.

We're not too far from my grandma's house,
who's here with us now,
whose home I assume we're going to,
at least for the night,
although I know we can't stay.

My grandmother's home has always been
a revolving door for any and everyone
who needs a place to stop over and stay awhile.

It is a single-story wood-paneled house

she proudly purchased in '95,

a single-story wood-paneled house

painted sage green

with dark forest-green trim,

sitting at the end of

a curved driveway

newcomers find easy to drive into

but need lots of practice

to back out of.

Mom moved in first with us back in 1995.

When she got on her feet,

we moved out and Mom's older sister, Lori,

came down from St. Louis

with her children, before she bought

a house of her own in Lithonia.

Since then,

it's been my grandmother's sister,

Aunt Gerald,

who came down from St. Louis one holiday

and decided to stay.

Aunt Gerald and my grandmother

are two peas in a pod,

like giggling schoolgirls,
constant companions,
who take pride in their churching,
in their watching over of the family
as joint matriarchs,
in their commanding of this house
and of this family.
They occupy the two back rooms.

The remaining two rooms,
the ones you pass first when
making your way
down that long hallway,
have been the rooms of children,
at times my siblings and me,
then Lori's children, our first cousins,
and now,
Grandma's and Auntie's oldest sons,
Donny and Ronnie,
as they cycle in and out,
as they've always done,
as we've come to imagine
they always will,
which is more than fine because usually,
we have a place of our own.

My grandmother's home has always been
a revolving door for any and everyone
who needs a place to stop over and stay awhile,
which means
there can't be much space for us now.

Who Even Knows

As Uncle Ronnie and Uncle Donny climb into the back
of Grandma's gray Nissan Maxima after a long day of
   helping
and lifting and moving and situating,
Mom hops out of the Mountaineer and speaks in
hushed tones to Grandma at her driver's-side window.

See y'all soon! Grandma loves you!
Grandma calls out as she pulls out of the parking lot.
I'm confused as to why she's telling us she loves us when
   we're
following her home
but quickly realize we're not actually
following her home
when we make a left out of the storage facility lot,
instead of the right she takes.

I eyeball Haley and then Josh,
expecting them to reveal whatever clues they may have
about where in the world we are headed,
but Josh
just shrugs
and Haley

rolls her eyes as if to say
Who even knows?

Before I know it,
we're back on 20,
this time headed back west toward the city,
taking the connector north to 85
and exiting at Buford Highway.

We're making a left on Sidney Marcus,
passing the apartment we lived in last summer,
the one where Dad moved in across the street
to be closer to us,
before he met his new wife
and moved to the suburbs.

We hop on 400 North,
hopping right back off at Exit 1, Lenox Road,
almost like we're headed back to our old apartment,
almost—
but we're not.

Family Friends

Instead,
we arrive in silence
at John and Carol's house—
Mom's friends,
family friends—
and for a split second,
I'm wondering if we're staying here for a while,
which would be *awesome*
because their house is *awesome*,
because their annual Thanksgiving gatherings are *awesome*
and I wonder what it'd be like to eat like that all the time,
or even just for a few days.

As we sit in the perfectly decorated den and watch TV,
eating on the food Ms. Carol has made,
I'm starting to get used
to the idea
that maybe, just maybe,
we'll be here for a while,
at least for the night,
until Mom steps into the room,
a bottle of wine in hand,
and says it's time for us to go.

Where are we going now? Haley boldly asks,
but Mom just cuts her eyes at her
which tells us
there simply isn't any more information for us
right now.

Starless Nights

Back in the Mountaineer,
an already-dark night growing darker,
we continue to drive.
And though we're not in the truck for long,
when you don't know where you're going,
a dark, starless road ahead
can seem painfully endless.

I write this in my notebook,
close it,
and settle in for the ride to
God knows where.

My Notebook

I like to play with words.
I take pride in discovering new words
I haven't heard before and
trying to figure out their meanings in context and
then being able to properly use them in future contexts,
both in school and
in everyday conversations.

New ways of knowing
and understanding
and feeling.

Words,
after all,
have power, and
there are so many I've still yet to discover,
which excites me and gives me hope
that there will always be new ways of knowing
and understanding,
and being.

In addition to capturing my thoughts and feelings,
I like to copy words into my journal,

words and quotes that speak to me,

that make me feel something,

that help me describe what I'm experiencing

in ways that assure me everything

will eventually

be okay

and even if it won't,

I still rejoice

knowing I still somehow found a way

to successfully name

what I was going through.

Hello, Disaster

We make our way back down Roswell Road,
past the Pearl Art & Craft Supplies store and
the Waffle House and Marcello's pizza,
past the Landmark Diner,
and make a right on West Paces Ferry Road,
driving, driving, driving,
past elegant homes that vary in style—
some old, some new,
some traditional, some modern,
but all sharing in their colossal size,

in their stately yards,
and perfectly illuminated driveways.

I wonder
about the people who live inside and
whether kids our age live there.

I wonder
about the kids who might live in these homes and
imagine they aren't the kinds of kids
who drive aimlessly in the dark,
wondering where they'll sleep at night.

I wonder

about the kids that might live in these homes and

imagine they aren't the kinds of kids

who say tearful goodbyes to their dogs at shelters,

and fearful *see you later*s to their belongings at storage units,

desperately hoping history won't repeat itself

but knowing better

than to ask God for a guarantee

that it won't.

I wonder

about the kids that might live in these homes and

imagine they aren't the kinds of kids

who just yesterday came home to

no lights,

no heat,

and fish who float upside down.

As my wonderings continue to stack

and pile on top of each other,

we make our way past the Governor's Mansion,

lined with what I assume are eight perfectly and routinely

pressure-washed white columns,

with its trio of flags,

some welcoming,

some not,

with a visitors' entrance that says
Come in
but a fully enclosed gate that says
Stay out.

We pass Pace Academy and
even more perfectly appointed homes
until we let out at Northside Parkway,
the OK Cafe to our left at the light,
which leads me to suck my teeth
at the sign that reminds me
that absolutely nothing
is okay tonight.

When the light turns green,
we continue straight ahead
where West Paces Ferry suddenly turns
into Paces Ferry,
curving to the right
and twisting and turning
past even more beautiful homes that lead me to build
even more elaborate stories about
the kinds of people who live there,
and what they may or
may not have to endure.

We pass the private school Lovett and cross over the
     Chattahoochee River
and before we know it,
the neighborhood very suddenly opens up again to
shops and stores and a sign that reads
Welcome to Vinings!

We pull over and right up to the entrance of a QuikTrip.
Mom hops out without a word
which means
she's hopping out to grab
her Benson & Hedges cigarettes,
with the distinct mint-green packaging
and gold trim.
Just as quickly as she's in,
she's back out and
we're back on the move again.
I have no idea where we are going
but figure we are about to jump
on the highway.

But instead of the highway,
we make a quick left immediately before the intersection,
weaving in and around a Walgreens parking lot
that sits next to a Kinko's,

before pulling into an empty space
in front of a four-story, brown-bricked building,
its face dotted with trees and shrubbery,
colossal in its own right but
far from the elegance we just passed through.
As Mom turns off the engine,
we turn in unison to see where we are,
slowly processing and reprocessing
the bright neon lights that meet our gaze:
EXTENDED STAY AMERICA.

Hello, disaster.

This Is It?

Ms. Lucille has always been
a guardian angel of sorts,
a family friend who appears in times of need,
which means
we must be in serious need tonight
if she is here with us
at this Extended Stay.

Hello, children,
Ms. Lucille says to us
in a voice that is distinctly kind
but also distinctly prehistoric,
a voice we imitate when she's out of earshot.
Though we chuckle between us,
we inevitably feel guilty for mocking
the voice of a woman who's
been nothing but doting,
in good times
and definitely in bad.

We manage lower-than-usual greetings in return,
too fixated on the four-story structure in front of us,

confused as to what this building could possibly have to do
with us.

We collect our bags from the trunk and ourselves,
what little of both we've been allowed to bring with us,
as Mom motions for us to follow her
through the glass-paneled doors,
pointing to the tan leather chairs inside,
which means
we are to take a seat.

We play musical chairs for the armchairs
to avoid the backless bench,
we line the walls of a lazily decorated lobby,
which sports red accent walls
and framed stock images of art
I'm convinced took
minutes to create.
Outside of us
and the front desk attendant,
there is no one in the lobby,
no other guests,
let alone children,
which makes me wonder,
what kind of place this is.

As we finish taking in
our limited surroundings,
which provide limited information
about where we are and why,
Mom and Ms. Lucille stand together
at the front desk.

We try our best to appear as if
we are minding our business,
but know that we are doing our best
to mind the business
that is Mom and Ms. Lucille
and the exchange of quiet whispers.

We can't gather much
but gather enough
when Ms. Lucille takes out cash,
as Mom signs a few pieces of paper,
and the front desk attendant points
in the direction of the elevators.

Once again,
we collect our bags and ourselves,
what little of both we've been allowed to bring with us,
as Ms. Lucille waves goodbye and
Mom motions for us to follow her.

We take the elevator to the third floor,
making our way down the twisting and turning
of quiet carpeted hallways until we find the door
that apparently is ours.

Mom uses a key card to open the door,
swinging it wide for all of us to step through.

I am relieved to see that the lights are on,
which I have to tell myself is not,
in fact,
a surprise because after all,
this is some sort of a hotel,
I think,
and hotels don't barter
with landlords over lights—
I think.

It is clean in a way even I can't appreciate,
sterile and smelling of the recent use
of disinfectants.

But this room doesn't have the *feel* of a hotel,
at least one that you'd actually want to stay in,
the kinds of hotels you'd hope to land in

if you were, perhaps,
visiting Disney World.

This hotel,
on the other hand,
houses a tiny kitchen
and a tiny beige-laminate desk with a singular white leg
that is attached to a wall,
a single queen-size bed,
topped with a white diamond-patterned quilt
and a brown bed skirt,
a television,
a phone,
a bathroom, and then,
and then,
that's it.

This room is sterile and unfixable,
at least in the ways
Mom has worked
to fix apartments
of the past.

There are more framed stock images
hanging above the bed

and in the bathroom,
a bathroom with a light
that when switched on
also automatically switches on
the dull whirring of an unseen fan.

I tell myself that we are somewhere
as opposed to nowhere
and that I should be grateful to have a place
to sleep at all tonight
but I'm too fixated on the tiny room in front us,
confused as to what it has to do with us.

This Is It

Where will we all sleep?
and
How long will we be here?
and
Where do we go from here?

These are questions I think to myself,
questions I don't dare answer
out of fear I'll anger my mom
or worse,
hurt her feelings.

Right on cue,
as if reading my mind,
Mom says,
It's just for a little while, okay?

Her voice is soft and kind
and full of what I think is
quiet shame, but if this is
the very best she could do tonight
and if this is the very best she could offer us tonight,
then this is more than okay with me—I think.

I nod to show that I hear her,
to show that I understand,
to show that I believe her.

Meanwhile, Josh rifles through his bag
for the PlayStation 2 he just got for Christmas,
while Haley picks up the remote
and plops down on the bed.

They offer nothing,
not even pretend,
no feigned belief
or acknowledgment
that anything at all
has been said.
This makes me so mad!
Why can't they see that she's trying?
Why can't they see that she's doing her best?

As we settle into this place,
there's a knock at the door,
a hotel employee with a rollaway bed,
I'm assuming is for Josh.
He's twelve, and it wouldn't make any sense
to make this already-torturous experience

more torturous by making him
sleep with his sisters and mother.

As Haley flips through the channels,
Josh starts to hook up his game
which means
a fight is coming
though I'm hoping
they have more sense tonight
than to bicker and brawl and
make tonight worse
than it already is.

I'll be back,
Mom says to no one in particular,
grabbing her cigarettes
and heading for the door.

There are two things Mom never brings into the house:
cigarettes and men,
though both linger on her when she returns.

I'm thankful for both,
though Lord knows I wish
she'd stop smoking.

Apocalypse

It's Sunday morning now,
which means
there's one more day
until the first day back to school
from winter break.

And though I'm excited to see James,
who I haven't really been able to talk to
this break since my phone got cut off,
I spend the whole day
praying for a miracle,
praying that we sleep
somewhere else tonight,
praying that we drive to school
from somewhere else,
anywhere else,
tomorrow morning.

We learn quickly that
children aren't allowed
in commons areas
unless accompanied
by an adult—

that this is a hotel for travelers and
serious people
with serious business and
serious homes to return to,

not families with no homes to return to—
which means
that because Mom spends most of the day
click-clacking away at the desktop computer we managed to
    bring,
working on her résumé and
applying for jobs,
we spend most of the day
in the room,
reading,
playing video games,
sleeping,
and watching TV.

There isn't much to say and
we try our best to stay out of each other's way,
still shell-shocked that this is where we are.

We share quesadillas for dinner
from the Willy's across the street
and I take longer than usual

blessing the food
for the miracle I fear
isn't coming tonight.

It's not so much
that being here
is the end of the world,
but somehow
the thought of going to school
from here,
the thought of carrying out
the very normal routine
that is going back to school
from this rather abnormal place,
feels apocalyptic.

As nighttime falls and
Mom insists on us
packing and repacking
our school bags
to ready ourselves for morning,
dread sets in as I realize
that my prayers won't be answered
tonight.

Here We Go, Again

It's Monday morning
and we four dance
an awkward dance,
struggling for our turn
in the bathroom,
since apparently
none of us thought it
wise to shower last night.

It is a most awkward dance of
twisting and turning to avoid collisions,
a terribly choreographed routine where we
pretend to offer each other privacy,
where there really isn't any to be found,
where we pirouette to offer access to the shower
when we're done.

We are tasked with the torture
of waiting,
collectively,
for each one of us to finish,
which gives us more time
than what I believe

is humanly necessary,

than what is simply humane,

to take in our fun-sized surroundings

that are not exactly fun.

We wait,

impatiently,

backpacks on backs,

avoiding the obvious

four corners of this tiny room,

watching the second episode

of *Saved by the Bell*,

which comes on

each morning at seven thirty a.m.,

a dire warning

that we're already running late

to school,

since we typically need to leave

no later than halfway through the

first episode to make it

in time.

Not to mention the fact that we are

outside the city limits now,

which means we are also

outside our school district.

I worry our school will find out about this,
though right now I'm fixated on the fact that
we should've been left to get there on time.

We pile into the truck and
begin the journey to school,
pulling out the lot and waiting at the
giant intersection,
285 and what we learn is the
giant corporate Home Depot complex to our left,
and the journey back to the city,
back to the end of the world,
to our right.

We amble back over Paces Ferry
to West Paces Ferry Road,
this time taking Northside Parkway
to Mount Paran,
to take in even more colossal homes
with what I imagine
are even more families
that I am convinced
don't have children
who make these kinds
of morning journeys to school.

Before we know it,
we pull into the car-pool line for school.
Josh and I step out of the truck
and eye the front entrance
of our middle school,
a massive brick complex
of blue-locker-lined hallways
and a series of complicated
stairwells that overflow with students.

Here we go,
I mumble to myself.

For me,
it is the second semester
of seventh grade,
and for Josh,
the second semester of sixth.

Haley stays with Mom.
She'll keep down Powers Ferry,
past Chastain Park, where
eons ago, we played Little League,
cutting across Roswell Road
and over to Old Ivy, where
she'll drop Haley off

for the first day
of her final semester at Sarah Smith,
our beloved elementary school.

It's Monday morning
and we two,
Josh and I,
are struggling to make our way
through the crowds
back into our middle school,
tasked with the torture of waiting,
collectively,
to see what the day holds
for each of us.

Ms. Lucca

Josh and I scurry to our homeroom classes to avoid late
    passes.
I barely slide into my seat and
catch the end of the roll call
(good fortune when your name falls at the end of the
    alphabet),
before the bell for first period rings and it's time to go to
    algebra,
an advanced math class seventh graders take with an eighth-
    grade teacher.
I amble up the stairs to the eighth-grade hall,
where Ms. Lucca's class sits at the end of the hallway,
stopping to talk to friends.
An administrator, Mr. Hill,
smartly though annoyingly guards the top of the stairs,
hurrying kids along and
breaking up hugs that linger too long.

I make it just in time.

Ms. Lucca's class
sits two floors

directly above the library

at the very end

of the eighth-grade hallway,

which means

an entire wall of windows,

which I sit against,

provides a similar,

though higher,

view of the outside world,

blessing us

with more sky

than concrete.

We sit in neat columns

that face forward,

Ms. Lucca's overhead projector

positioned in the front

for models and guided practices

that assure any and everyone

who steps through her doors

that they, too,

are capable mathematicians,

and not just math savant Emil,

whose intellect *should* be intimidating

(considering he reads math books for fun)

but isn't,
since his sense of humor and good heart
make it impossible to ever feel small.

Ms. Lucca has the brain of a planner
but the heart of a pantser.

We joke with her and
she jokes back,
never taking herself
or us
too seriously,
until we've clowned too much—
    like the time we all agreed to drop our pencils on the floor
    at the exact same time or
    the day we all jumped out of our seats in unison
    and started singing "I Ran" by Flock of Seagulls,
and she has
to bring it back
with a seriousness
that is equally jarring
and commanding of respect—

After all,
she is unequivocally herself

and gives us space to be ourselves, too—
and we love her for it.

But though I am overjoyed
to see her bright and early
this first Monday morning
back to school,
anxiety swells in my throat
as I take my seat
by the window.

After all,
Maia sits two rows over
and we don't speak,
let alone meet eyes,
not even once.

There Are Few Pains

more painful
than not being on
speaking terms
with your best friend.

Though we'd seen each other around,
Mai and I officially met
in the bathroom
last year,
the one at the end
of the Power Team hallway.
It was Spirit Week,
and more specifically,
Hat Day,
and I told her I liked her hat,
and she told me she liked mine, too.

That summer,
which was last summer,
we were inseparable,
when life at home was less complicated.
We spent hot days
roaming Six Flags alone,

convincing our mothers
to let us have at it, alone.
We were happy without parents and annoying younger
    siblings,
spending summer evenings
watching movies at Phipps
and dancing silly dances
in the entrance halls
until we erupted
with deep belly laughter,
until one of our mothers
came to pick us up.

We bonded over our perspectives
and our shared love of books and music.
She has the craziest CD collection,
complete with everything
old and new,
like New Edition
and Sade
and Aaliyah (her favorite)
and Amerie.

I attended my first concert with her,
Nelly and Jagged Edge,
and we sat second row

thanks to her aunt.

We screamed together at the Scream II tour,

and we rejoiced at the

start of seventh grade,

when she joined

first-period algebra

with Ms. Lucca,

where we

made funny faces and

traded elaborate notes,

mutually overjoyed

that we have each other,

that we aren't alone,

especially considering

we are the only two

Black girls

in this class.

She is fearless

and proud and encourages me

to be the same.

With her,

I can never

be alone.

But things change
when I get my first
"real" boyfriend.

More and more,
I start to leave
her alone,
my neediness kneading me
into something I don't want to be
but don't know how not to be,
just yet.

But things change most
when she proves
that she's always had my back,
more than I've been capable
of having my own.

James

He is an escape—
a way away from chaos,
a way to feel loved
and heard, too.

We met at the beginning of this school year through Zahra,
one of my eighth-grade friends who insisted the cute
    eighth-grade boy I'd been noticing
had been noticing me, too—
even though it seemed there were always other girls
he was noticing too.

We connected fast
And soon began talking in the halls
and passing notes.

We can talk for hours about nothing
and do,
much to the dismay of my parents
(who agreed for once by saying I'm too young),
and my teachers
(who say he's such a distraction),
and my friends

(who wonder where their friend has gone
when I start to spend all my spare time
with him).

Even though he's not the best student
and gets in trouble a lot at school
(more cause for teachers to wonder what I see in him),
he writes me poetry
and listens when I'm happy
or sad,
or frustrated,
or excited—
which makes me feel more seen
than how I'd feel
without him.

Pre-Calculations

In my opinion, there are three kinds of teachers in this world:
The ones who fly by the seat of their pants, whose classrooms
    always smell like last-minute,
frantically made copies,
the ones with meticulous plans who use every last second of
    class as if their very lives
depended on it,
and the ones who are clearly recycling material they
    "perfected" twenty years ago,
who make minimal efforts to make class interesting or fresh.

There are pros and cons to each one.

If the pantsers are fun and down-to-earth,
they'll tell great stories and you'll get to talk to your friends.
It'll be easy to distract them from teaching
because they don't really have a plan to teach
in the first place—
which, in my opinion,
is a win-win.

On the other hand,
there's a good chance you'll end up watching –

lots and lots of boring movies,

which wouldn't be *that* bad

if they didn't come with stupid, pointless questions

that feel more like busywork

than anything useful.

You'll never go over the answers

or see the "grade," which

makes me think these are balled up

and thrown in the trash, so

why even bother?

Then you have the planners,

the strict and unrelenting teachers

who wake up in the morning wondering

how best to torture you next.

In their classes,

you won't be able to get away with much,

not talking,

or journaling,

or burying your nose in a new favorite book but—

you might actually learn something

and you might actually feel proud of yourself

when and if you get a good grade on an assignment.

Earning an A in this class

with this kind of teacher

will feel like taking home a gold medal in the Olympics
BUT
the work is brutal, which leads to
the constant rolling of my eyes,
which at some point,
I'm told,
will cause them to get stuck to the back of my head—
a chance I'm willing to take because someone
has to know this is the worst!!
(but also, secretly, the best)

Finally, there are the OG's,
the ones convinced they figured everything out forever ago
and never need to update anything,
whose faded copies look as if they were originally
    typewritten.

With these teachers,
I'm confident I could write down
just about anything and get full credit,
extra credit, even.
After all,
the more nonsense you write, the better,
and if there is one thing I'm good at writing,
it's nonsense.

My seventh-grade teachers are a combination of all three,
and some of them are combinations in and of themselves.
And though you *may* think that I have a preference,
you *may* be surprised to learn that right now,
that variety is actually quite helpful because right now,
I can pick and choose when I am *on* and when I am *off*,
pre-calculating the mental and emotional energy
I might need to exert one given period to the next,
pre-calculating when I might actually have to work and
pre-calculating when I can c o a s t.

And right now,
I need all the coasting I can get.

How Was Your Break?

The rest of the day is a blur,
as the world still spins.
There are still
locker combinations
to spin and homework
to be done.
There's still the god-awful
beeping of the pacer test
and tortured science lessons
about dominant and recessive traits.
There are still rigid rules
to follow about when to speak and
when and how
to raise your hand to go to the bathroom and
I tell myself over and over again
that we are not special,
that your mom being in between jobs,
again,
is not special,
that staying in a hotel
is not special,
that if the world stopped every time
something bad happened to anyone,

the
world would
never
move.

But God how I
wish it'd slow down
sometimes, lest I
fall down and off
and into outer space.
And God how I wish
friends would stop
asking how my
winter break was.

After all, I don't
think people *really* care
to know how you're *really*
feeling when they fix
their mouths to ask you
how you're doing.
They can't possibly
mean it, right?
After all,
it's just a gesture, right?
It's just a greeting,

meant to be quick

and casual and a segue

to more interesting conversations,

more enjoyable conversations,

conversations that don't

cause immediate discomfort,

that don't spark immediate

awkward silences and

pathetic offerings of

I'm so sorry because

what do they even

have to be sorry for?

So instead of

blurting out

A total disaster

and

We lost our dog

and *The guts of Josh's fish*

are probably still festering

in the apartment carpet

downstairs right now,

right as we speak

and

To make matters worse,

we moved into an

Extended Stay
and
I have no earthly idea how long we'll be there
and
I'm sharing a bed
with my eleven-year-old
sister and my mom,
who won't stop
crying
and
I can't even hear
myself think
and
I wish that I
could fly away—
I pause,
take a deep breath,
and say
It was great, Alana!
How was yours?

After all,
I don't think my other friend Alana would understand what
    I'm going through.
I don't think she could understand.

Not when her life exists the way it does,

with parents who live together

and individual rooms for her and her sisters,

with mealtimes that are never questioned,

let alone overlooked.

"Family Friends"

Later in the day,
in Ms. Jackson's social studies class,
I read and reread
the many posters on her wall,
so-called motivational posters
that say things like

> *Hard work spotlights the character of people:*
> *some turn up their sleeves,*
> *some turn up their noses,*
> *and some don't turn up at all.*

I take out my journal,
the one where I word-vomit my thoughts
and copy song lyrics and quotes,
and copy this one too,
though I have changes
I'd like to suggest,
something along the lines of

> *Hard times spotlight the true value of "family friends":*
> *some turn up their sleeves,*

some turn up their noses,
and some don't turn up at all.

Oh, and

some send you off with a "good luck"
and a smile
that is supposed to be comforting and reassuring,
but isn't.

Almost Doesn't Count

After school almost feels normal
and I almost forget that we don't have a home—
though I'm quickly reminded
when instead of making a right out of the school parking lot
and heading back to the apartment on Roswell Road,
we make a left and begin to twist and turn
our way back to the hotel,
repassing homes with all their possibilities
that right now
don't feel possible for us.

Songs in A Minor

Back at the hotel,
the business of dinner and homework
still needs doing,
despite the fact that this regular Monday night
feels anything but normal.

We grab slices of pizza
from the box Mom ordered and
branch off into what
crevices of the room
we're able to carve out
for ourselves
and get to work.

Sitting at the tiny desk,
I shuffle through my bag
for my homework folders
and my journal,
unwrap my headphones,
and press play on the
Songs in A Minor CD
I've been wearing out
since I first got it

the summer after fifth grade.
As "Piano & I" begins to play,
I start to relax a little.
This feels normal,
music and homework and
headphones that let you tune out
everyone and everything,
despite the fact that this regular Monday night
is anything but normal.

Control Freak

I can't say that I understand the point
of homework in the first place,
but there should absolutely positively be a rule
against doing homework
when you have hard stuff going on
at home.

I'm still at this tiny desk
after Haley and Josh
have long since called it quits,
giving all the time they're willing to give
to their homework tonight.

Meanwhile,
I am staring down an assignment for drama class—
who even gave drama permission to assign homework??—
an assignment I was *supposed* to work on
over the recent winter break,
back when we still had space to stretch out
and focus,
but of course,
I put it off
and now I'm sitting at this tiny desk,

staring down this assignment for drama class
that is due tomorrow.

We've been studying *The Miracle Worker*,
which makes Helen Keller out to be a brat
who demands control of everything
and everyone around her,
entirely different from the Helen Keller
I've grown up learning about in school.
I am both intrigued and disgusted,
inspired and irritated.

For this assignment,
I'm *supposed* to define a set of vocabulary words.
I'm *supposed* to summarize scenes and write responses
and come up with something called "inspirational creative
    writing,"
but to be honest, I'm not exactly feeling inspired right now.
I skip over the vocabulary when I remember
that's the section that counts least.
Let's be real: when you have one night
to complete two weeks' worth of work,
you have to be strategic.

So instead,
I spend time poring over the summaries

and pondering my responses
and wouldn't you know it—
by the time I need to complete the "inspirational creative
    writings,"
they end up going much faster than I expected,
ultimately ending up being pseudo diary entries
for what is happening right now,
like how annoying my siblings are and
how I wish they'd get with the program,
my program, that is.

At this point,
I have "Troubles" on repeat.
As Alicia Keys sings what I feel,
I write things like
Annie went through a troubling
and hard childhood,
like I seem to be
experiencing now—
but stop short of
giving specifics, because
the last thing anyone needs
is teachers asking questions,
poking and
prodding and
demanding details

all because you
poured your heart out into your homework
and came to school crying the next day
asking for a snack.

Besides,
I remind myself that
we are not special,
that having a mother
who cycles in and out of employment
is not special
that belonging to a family
that cycles in and out of housing
is not special,
that not having money
is not special,
that mismanaging money
is certainly not special.

But again,
as the night goes on and
everyone starts to climb into bed,
when the lights are switched off and
I'm still sitting here
at this tiny desk,
still working,

I am reminded

that I wholeheartedly believe

that there should absolutely positively be a rule

against doing homework

when you have hard stuff going on at home.

Better yet, there should absolutely positively be a rule

against doing homework

when you don't have a home to begin with.

Six p.m. on Friday

The rest of the week inches and zooms,
zooms and inches,
with promises from Mom that
we'll have this figured out soon,
and before we know it,
it's Friday afternoon and
we've somehow survived.

After all,
the world doesn't stop spinning
just because your world currently makes no sense,
just because you're currently holed up in a hotel
and struggling to find time and space to think.

We barely have enough time to catch our breath
before it's six p.m. and like clockwork,
Dad's downstairs,
ready to pick us up
for the weekend.

Every Other Weekend

Dad gets us every other weekend,
per the custody agreement.
It's been this way for years,
ever since Mom and Dad split up
centuries ago, and
I guess I'm lucky that I'm
not one of those kids
who spends years in therapy
because they're still devastated
their parents went their separate ways.

And though I know the divorce was harder
on my father than it was for my mother—
after all,
he'll tell you himself
that because he was willing to stay,
she should have been willing to stay, too,
that he wanted more than anything for her to stay, too—
I don't have any memories of my parents together,
and to be honest,
knowing how different they are,
I have a hard time imagining a time
when they could have even

been together,
at all.

Their stories change,
but what I've gathered
is that Dad was a worker,
too careful and too practical,
and Mom was a dreamer,
too ambitious and too fantastical—
and somewhere in all of that,
it no longer made sense to stay together.

I wonder if they were pretending or
if they changed or
if they knew all along that it wouldn't work
but tried anyway.

Sometimes I think I want to know
but then again,
I've never known them together.
Their divorce was finalized on my fifth birthday.
I know because I saw the paperwork, and
despite my efforts to convince myself
that that was a tragedy worth mourning,
I couldn't because
in reality,

it wasn't.
In reality,
it was more like a fun fact
that wasn't fun at all.

For the most part,
they get along
and make the business
of raising us separately
work,
at least
that's what we see.

On more than one occasion,
they've rented apartments in complexes
across the street from one another,
which made weekend exchanges a breeze.

Once,
Dad even moved into the basement
of a house we were renting,
and that worked too.

But I know better
than to think their relationship is all good.
After all,

they're so, so different—
even beyond the obvious,
with Mom being Black and Dad being white—
but I'm nonetheless convinced
they do a great job
of hiding whatever disagreements
they might have from us.

There are no screaming matches,
no idle threats,
no real threats,
just looks between them
that tell anyone who's watching closely
that they too wonder
how they ever managed
to get together,
let alone stay together,
long enough
to have us.

To the Suburbs

We meet Dad in the parking lot,
backpacks slung over our shoulders,
loading them up
and then ourselves,
into his white Ford pickup truck.
But instead of an apartment complex
across the street
or even across town,
we begin the forty-minute drive
outside the perimeter
as the sun sets
to the suburbs,
to Lawrenceville,
which might as well
be the middle of absolute nowhere—
to three kids who have spent
most of their lives moving all over
the city of Atlanta—
within 285, the highway that circles the city, that is—
where Dad bought a new house last year
with a new wife

who speaks a new language
we don't know
and don't care to learn
just yet.

Brick Walls

Ning is a quiet woman,
dainty in size
but commanding
of their house and
most definitely
of my father.

Though she has been in America for some time now,
she is from Thailand and
her English is sparse.

We have our questions
and wonder how *this*
is supposed to work,
though Dad is clearly overjoyed
by *this*,
floating in an extended fog
of honeymoon bliss
that I try to convince myself
is what matters most,
even if *this* seems to matter most,
even above us,
his children.

Not to mention,
I don't think *this*
is what Ning signed up for—
three Black stepchildren and their moody mother,
and though it hasn't been said,
I wonder if she wonders why Dad bothers
to care for a child that's not his own,
which makes me wonder if Haley's been wondering the same.

I don't want to believe that, though,
and try to convince myself that she's nice enough,
even through the uncertainties,
even if we find her ways to be strange,
like offerings to Buddhist gods
adorning the living room
next to framed photos of
white Jesus,
even if she wears pants
in unbearable Georgia summers,
even if we don't have much to talk about,
even if the silences between us
when Dad briefly leaves a room
are brick walls.

Blockbuster

The drive up 85 North,
away from the city
and all that we know,
is never particularly festive,
but it's quieter tonight,
and none of us kids
are that interested in talking
much about the kind of week we've had.

Dad doesn't seem to notice,
per usual,
and cracks his corny Dad jokes,
per usual,
looking for a laugh
or maybe even a smile.

We don't have much for
him right now,
but I'm sure that'll change
when we get to his house
and get settled.

After more awkward silence,
he turns up the radio on Star 94,
his favorite station.
I hate country music
and would be happier
if he'd at least put the Chicago tape on,
their *Greatest Hits, 1982–1989*, that is,
the one that starts with "Hard to Say I'm Sorry,"
the one that would be a
welcome compromise,
but I don't have the energy
to try to convince him to play
anything else right now.

And perhaps he is looking
for a protest,
anything that shows
proof of life from the
quieter-than-usual children
he is shuttling to the suburbs,
to Lawrenceville,
to what might as well be
the middle of absolute nowhere,
but right now,

I can't even muster
my typical eye roll.

How about Wendy's? Dad asks
as he turns down the radio and
we finally pull off the highway
at Sugarloaf Parkway.

It's a weekend tradition that none of us
are going to pass on,
a welcome reprieve from
questions and country music.

After collecting bags of burgers and fries
and trays of Frostys at the window,
Dad cuts across the parking lot
and pulls into a space
in front of Blockbuster,
another weekend tradition.

Armed with already-melting Frostys and French fries,
we barrel out of the car
and roll into the store,
breaking off into different directions
to find a movie for the weekend.

We know the drill: we're here for two movies
and two movies only.
One will be Dad's choice
(with a high chance it'll be a kung fu movie),
and the other will be our collective choice.

This is the way it's always been, and though
this is always hard to do, we somehow
always figure it out, knowing
there's no way in the world
Dad is going for a third,
let alone a fourth,
movie.

We pace up and down the fully stocked aisles,
sometimes meeting each other at the ends,
equipped with options and suggestions,
ready to exchange *I don't think so*s and
We just watched that one last month.

Finally, after tense negotiations,
we settle on *Blue Streak*,
meeting back up at the front of the store
after Dad makes his infamous animal call,
a mix between a hyena, a hippo, and a canary,

a signal we've always known means,
Come find me.

When we were younger,
we loved this sound
and struggled to no avail to figure out
how to make it ourselves,
gleefully running to meet our dad
at the front of wherever we were,
but

as we've gotten older,
it makes us roll our eyes in contempt
wishing he'd find some other,
much more normal way of letting us know
it's time to go.

At the register,
as we wait for Dad to pull out
his Blockbuster card and cash to pay,
I spoon the last few bites of my Frosty
into my mouth,
ditching the empty cup in the trash,
which sits next to a stack
of the latest editions of *Apartment Guide.*

On the way out the door,
I swipe one
and start flipping through the pages
as we head toward the truck.
On the short drive home,
Dad is talking
a million miles a minute
and asking a thousand questions
about what we want to do this weekend,
even though we will do what we always do.
I'm lost in the pages
of the thick book,
hoping to land
on a reasonable apartment
located within a reasonable distance
of our school district
that will make much more sense
than this hotel we've landed at.

If I can't control *when* we'll move or *how*,
I demand to have a say in *where*.

No Shoes in the House

We roll our eyes in unison
but dutifully pull off our shoes
and leave them in the garage.

After all,
Dad doesn't have to remind us
and we are confused
as to why he feels the need
to tell us every time we come over,
as if we've never been to the house
he shares with his beloved Ning before,
as if we've ever even had the opportunity
to break this precious rule,
or any of the countless others,
before.

We've just pulled in to Dad's house,
which sits at the front of a well-appointed subdivision,
where all the homes essentially look the same,
a mix of white paneling and brick.

We always enter through the garage
and never through the front door,

which sports extra locks and extra bolts
in the event someone dares to be extra bold
and try to break in.

Dad believes in security, and all the windows
in this home sport similar locks and alarms
to ensure that intruders stay out,
though I sometimes wonder
if they're also meant
to keep us in.

We step in through the garage door
and throw our bags in the downstairs guest room,
the one with collages of our childhood photos
hung on the walls,
the one with the brown pullout couch
we'll all sleep on later tonight,
the same pullout couch
we've been sleeping on together
whenever we've visited Dad's
on the weekends,
for years.

Before,
when Dad lived in one-bedroom apartments
in the city by himself,

or even in the one-room apartment above the garage
on Mr. Lawrence's farm—
the lawyer from the country club
who represented him during the
divorce trial,
to repay the debt
for the representation
he couldn't afford—
this made sense.

But now,
he and Ning have two empty,
unfurnished bedrooms upstairs,
bedrooms I'm convinced
could easily be converted into rooms for us three,
but for some reason
aren't.
Counting this guest room,
each of us could technically
even have
our own room,
which would be new for us anytime
but especially deeply appreciated
right now
considering where we've recently landed
with Mom.

But each time I ask
about these rooms,
I get a different answer,
a different reason,
a different explanation
that ultimately circles back to the point
that we are sleeping in this guest room,
on this brown pullout couch
together,
as we've always done,
throughout the years,
which makes less and less sense,
if you ask me,
considering I am thirteen now,
Josh is twelve, and Haley is eleven.

I convince myself
it's better to sleep down here
anyway, because
at least we have the TV
and the movies
and the games
and the only evidence
of modern-day life
in this house.

The rest of the house,
on the other hand,
looks like an off-limits museum
meets a Sam's Club warehouse
meets a nondenominational,
cross-religion sanctuary.

In the living room,
there are brand-new couches
covered in quilts
meant to keep them clean
and free of dirt and grime
that sit in front of a
wall-to-wall mahogany entertainment center
that covers a cable-less TV
and rows of rows of Dad's collectibles—
twenty-two model Harley-Davidsons
and animated figurine sets
that Dad locates on
antique store adventures.

Over the fireplace,
there hang framed portraits
of the king and queen of Thailand,
with offerings to Buddhist gods,
a glass of water here,

a tray of flowers there,

lining the white mantel.

Dad's framed photo of white Jesus

still hangs on the horizontal ceiling pillar

separating the living room from the kitchen,

reassuring evidence that Ning

is not interested in changing

everything.

In the kitchen closets and cupboards,

there are endless stockpiles

of dried foods and other goods

that make me think

Dad and Ning

are preparing for a disaster

only they can see coming,

which mirror other closets

throughout the house

that similarly house

stores of toilet paper

and paper towels

and laundry detergent

and soaps

that make me wonder

what Dad and Ning believe is coming.

Then again,
Dad has always believed in
being prepared, and it's a
welcome reprieve
from the certain uncertainty
that is Mom's house.

Stacks of work polos
and dress pants sit in baskets
on the laundry room floor,
the one that sits in between
the guest room and the kitchen,
where plastic containers of cut fruit,
mixed salads,
and meal-prepped lunches and dinners
wait for my dad,
for work
and for when he's home from work
and Ning is not there.

She goes above and beyond
to make sure he is always prepared,
to make sure he is always ready,
for work and the life
they've made for themselves
out here in the suburbs,

in Lawrenceville,
which might as well
be the absolute middle of nowhere,
to us.

This fairly new house is one
of mutual compromise and respect,
of mutual love and dependency,
for a fairly newly wed couple
who spend their days and nights
working
and any parts of their days and nights
not working,
preparing for work,
fawning over each other,
or sleeping.

And because every moment of their
waking lives seems to be
so very highly intentional,
I come to believe that
despite the *appearance* of
two empty, unfurnished bedrooms upstairs,
perhaps Dad and Ning
have other plans that involve
more careful preparation

for whatever else
they believe is coming
to the house
they've clearly established
for only themselves.

And though I've never felt
particularly at home here,
I nonetheless find it nice
to be in a house at all,
with multiple rooms
that have multiple doors
that shut,
with multiple bathrooms
and multiple spaces
and multiple corners
to hole up in,
to find some semblance of privacy
after a week of
having none.

We plop down on the brown couch
and pop in *Blue Streak*.
We watch it together,
us four,
like we always do.

And when it's over,
we pull out the cushions
and unfold the dark
metal frame and pull
the fitted sheets
over the corners of the mattress
and grab the pillows
and blankets
from the closet,
like we always do,
and curl up
as best we can so as
to give each other some .
semblance of space
in our respective corners—
Haley, per usual,
suffering in the middle
because she is the baby
and that's just the
way it is—
and try to fall asleep
despite the growing anger
I feel inside
that despite the multiple rooms
in this home,
we are still sleeping

together as if we are young children,

as if we are still living in a one-bedroom apartment,

as if we are still at the Extended Stay hotel with Mom.

But even before this week,

this is the way it's always been, and though

this is always hard to do,

we somehow always figure it out, knowing

there's no way in the world

Dad is giving us those

extra, empty,

unfurnished bedrooms

upstairs.

Always Together

It's Saturday morning,
which means a big breakfast
with Dad and Ning.

This, I like.

And even though they don't believe
in seasoning their food,
the scrambled eggs, Pillsbury Grands! biscuits,
sliced ham, and cheese grits
are nevertheless appreciated.

Ning asks us what we want to drink,
which is the most conversation
we will have this morning.

After breakfast,
Ning clears the table
and does the dishes.
We aren't allowed to help,
which is great
and weird
at the same time.

Over the years,
Dad has shared tidbits
about living in poverty with
a maniacal stepfather,
enabled by a bystander mother,
about all the grueling domestic work
he and his six siblings
were forced to do,
among other things
he can't put into words.
He stops short of sharing more and
says that's why he doesn't want us
to clean up around the house.
That we are guests in this home,
which seems great at first,
but the word "guests" leaves a bad taste in my mouth
and reminds me why I can never feel at home here.

We'd all like to spend the day
lying around the house,
Haley watching movies or
Josh playing computer games or
me talking to James on the phone,
but Dad insists that Saturdays are for Sam's Club—
all together.

And so we pile into
Ning's pristine burgundy
Toyota Camry,
the one that still looks and smells
like it just rolled off
a dealership lot,
since we can't all fit in Dad's pickup,
and take off toward Sam's.

There's a part of me
that appreciates how much "family time"
Dad wants to spend with us
considering he only sees us
every other weekend,
   fondly remembering the days
   we spent tossing baseballs
   in empty fields,
   running through Six Flags together
   in coordinated outfits,
   or learning how to swim
   at the public pool at Chastain,
but there's the other part of me
that absolutely hates it.

I'm thirteen years old
and would like more independence!

Instead,
we're being herded around Gwinnett County
like elementary school kids,
struggling for space
and air to breathe
as we sit side by side
in the back seat of
Ning's pristine burgundy Toyota Camry.

This, I don't like.

Sam's Club

We walk together at Sam's,
as usual,
watching Dad and Ning
meticulously grab items
from their pre-prepared shopping list,
as usual.

They are two kids in love,
which makes us their
third,
fourth,
and fifth wheels.

While they compare prices
and freshness
and bargains
and value,
we happily stand in line
and accept samples from attendants
who are eager to disperse
what they cook at their stands.
Dad, let's get this one!
we say when we stumble across something

particularly interesting and tasty.
We are dismayed
by Dad's refusal
to buy anything that is not on his list,
anything that has not been pre-planned and pre-budgeted
    for,
but we are not surprised
because *this* is standard.

Dad's always been careful with his money
but he and Ning live by an excruciatingly strict budget,
at least by the standards
of preteen children
who want things.
They painstakingly consider every purchase,
together,
take great pleasure in finding great deals,
together,
and bask in activities like
window-shopping at the mall,
which is essentially every preteen's worst nightmare.

We toss our findings
back in the giant freezers
where they came from
and continue to begrudgingly

follow Dad and Ning around the store
as they continue checking items off their list.
We are relieved
when it is finally time to leave,
impatiently waiting in line
as items are individually scanned
and they work together
to bag and box their bounty.
Before we know it,
we are back in the pristine Camry
and heading home,
another relief given the fact
that after we pull back into the garage
and get everything inside,
we'll be able to separate again
and find our own ways
to pass the rest of the afternoon,
alone.

There's a loophole in "together time":
We usually return to the house around noon,
which means we'll have
a few hours to ourselves
while Dad dotes on Ning
before she leaves for her restaurant job at two p.m.,
as usual.

He treats this time with her
as if it's the last time he'll see her
before she departs for a very, very long journey,
even though she'll be home by eleven,
as usual.

Adorable, right?
Actually, I feel like vomiting,
but it is a welcome reprieve
because come two p.m., it's back to "family time,"
as usual.

Why Can't We Stay Here?

Later that night,
after hours of getting lost in a book,
of playing solitaire
and rewatching old movies,
Dad pulls out his giant Monopoly game,
the collector's item he says
took a year's worth of payments to pay off.
We're slow to admit it,
but we love playing Monopoly together
and excitedly rush to get it set up
and lay claim to the pieces
we'll play with.

Before you know it,
we're laughing as we
competitively argue
about whose turn it is to not pass go,
whose turn it is to collect two hundred dollars,
whose turn it is to go straight to jail.

As we play,
we eat freeze pops
by the handful,

collecting cash
and properties
until it's late,
until Dad says it's time to lie down,
which at thirteen,
sounds like a punishment.

Even still,
we dutifully head to the guest room, and
as Dad pulls out the couch and
grabs the sheets to make the bed,
a part of me can't help but wonder
why we can't live here until Mom gets back on her feet,
even though there would be clear trade-offs.

I wonder if it's the drive.
After all,
we are *really* far from the city,
and I imagine it'd be hard
to get us to school
in the mornings.
Dad's job starts at four thirty in the morning
at the country club in Midtown and
his evening shift at the shipping hub back up 85 at four,
which already demands shuttling

in and out of Atlanta commuter traffic
and would undoubtedly
be made more complicated
if that commute involved additional stops.

No doubt he'd have to take us to work with him,
then leave work,
to take me and Josh to school
and then Haley to hers,
then back to work,
and who even knows how the afternoons
would possibly work,
since he's not off again
until the following morning.

I don't see that happening.

But what about Ning?

In my opinion,
this would be a great opportunity
for her to showcase
her commitment to her
stepmotherly duties,
for her to show

that she is just as dedicated
to our day-to-day lives
as she shows she is
to our father's.

Plus, I know there are other kids
whose families live outside the district
but whose families still make a way for them
to get to school every day.

Surely they could do it too, right?

I keep most of my conclusions
to myself but blurt out,
Dad, why can't we stay here?

Dad doesn't pause or even look up,
instead continuing
to pull the fitted sheet
around the mattress
we'll sleep on together
tonight.

Ask your Mom, he says.
I've offered, but she said no.

So it isn't the drive,
I think to myself,
as we climb into bed.

That night,
after Haley and Josh are sound asleep,
I lie awake staring into the darkness,
wondering why Mom
won't let us go.

Running Starts

In my dreams,
I can fly.
In my dreams,
I can go wherever I like
and do whatever I please,
which is much, much different
than my everyday waking,
walking life.

In my dreams,
I can fly,
but I have to get a good running start first,
otherwise,
I won't be able
to gather the proper momentum
needed to propel myself
into flight
and stay there.

At the first sign of trouble,
I'm out.
I have no interest

tonight, or any night,

in battling shape-shifting demons and

I don't trust that my weapons will materialize when they
   need to,

even if we are operating in a dreamworld,

even if I should be able to manifest what I need,

at the precise moment I need it.

And so at the first sign of trouble,

I take off and up and out of the universe,

quite literally,

propelling myself through time and space and other worlds

until I find the mystical,

the magical,

and the safe.

More often than not,

these spaces are abandoned—

floating windowless and doorless castles,

enchanting seaside villages with homes that freckle cascading
   hills,

rich forest expanses that curtain crystal clear waters.

More often than not,

I explore these spaces alone, but sometimes,

sometimes trouble follows,
threatening to catch up,
to catch me and yank me back.

In these dreams,
I struggle to control my direction.
I lean one way and find myself pulled in another.
As I steer toward the fantastical,
I might be pulled toward something different,
something darker,
something stronger than me,
threatening to take me somewhere
I don't want to go.

And even if I manage to break away,
flight proves exhausting
and sooner or later,
whether I want to or not,
I find myself falling
back to the ground.

What am I avoiding in the sky tonight,
and every night?
Everything.

My landings are always smooth,

although I may not land where I want to be.

I can escape all things bad—

cops and robbers and shape-shifting monsters, too—

but once again,

if I don't get that proper running start,

I'm not going anywhere.

Mom's Going to Be Pissed

It's Sunday night
and we're back in
the Extended Stay hotel
parking lot.

As Dad hands us
our bags from the
bed of his truck,
he reaches in and
grabs two last totes
I didn't quite
notice before.

What's this? I ask,
peering inside.

Food, for the room,
he says.

I manage to utter a nervous thanks
as he moves to hug us all
before sending us upstairs.

It's six o'clock on the dot
and per usual,
Dad's timing is
impeccable.

See you soon,
he calls out,
as he pulls his
truck out of the
lot to leave.

I pause and
consider the
weight of what
I'm holding.

A bundle of bananas.
A gallon of milk.
A loaf of bread.
Sandwich meat.

There's more, and
these are good things,
I know,
but somehow this

just doesn't feel
right.

After all,
we're still
at this hotel
and Dad is still
going back to his house,
the one that still
has the two empty,
unfurnished bedrooms
upstairs.

Perhaps there is more
to this than I can possibly
understand right now.

Perhaps I'm missing
the bigger picture
or simply wouldn't
get it.

Or,

perhaps
I'm simply having a very

hard time wrapping
my head around the idea
that Dad basically handed
us a bag full of charity,
essentially told us,
Good luck!
before skirting out of
the parking lot
and back up to
Lawrenceville,
back to his beloved
wife, Ning, and the
two empty, unfurnished
bedrooms upstairs.

I don't know
which one is right to feel,
but what I *do* know is that
Mom's going to be pissed.

And She Is.

At first, she's all smiles and
happy to see us when she hears
our knocks and opens
the door—
a welcome change from
last week's sadness
and despondency—

but her smile quickly
disappears when she
peeks her head into
the bags I've placed
on the kitchen counter.

What's this? she asks.

Before I can decide how
exactly I want to explain
what's in the bags,
before I can decide how
exactly I want to phrase it
to minimize the impact

and keep her from snapping,
Haley matter-of-factly says,
Groceries.
Dad said he wanted to make sure
we had food for the week.

There goes Haley again,
never failing to say exactly what she means
and meaning exactly what she says.

I am terrified just
as much as I am
in awe.

Is that right?
Mom says,
cocking her head to the side.

She lets out a light chuckle,
but I know very well from
experience that she doesn't
find any of this to be funny.

Time slows as she pulls
each item out of the bag,

meticulously studying
each item before lining
each item up on the kitchen counter.

In addition to the bread
and the sandwich meat
and the cereal
and the milk,
there are also boxes of spaghetti
and jars of spaghetti sauce,
a few cans of green beans,
packs of ramen
and that bunch of bananas.

I bet all this came from his kitchen,
Mom says to no one in particular.

I bet he thinks he's doing us a real big favor,
sending y'all back with food like this,
instead of more money.

Dad drops off child support every Thursday at six p.m.,
so this "extra money" Mom thinks he might offer?
Please!
Even I know that's not happening.

Thinking back to the fish tank,
I'm half expecting her to trash it all,
but she doesn't.

Instead,
she puts the cold items
in the refrigerator
and leaves everything else out
on the counter,
as if to say,
Do with it what you must.

I'll be back,
she says,
grabbing her coat and
scraping her cigarettes
and the key card from the desk.

So much for being happy to see us.

As the door closes behind her,
I let out the breath I've been holding.

What's her problem?
Why is she trippin'?
Haley asks, to no one in particular.

Josh shrugs.
You know how she can be,
he says,
focused on starting his game up.

I suck my teeth
and ignore them both,
eyeing the food on the counter.
I am annoyed they can't see
that Mom feels insulted
and they don't want to do anything
to make it better.

I don't know how long Mom
will be gone, but
I'm intent on making sure
that when she returns,
everything is cleaned up
and put away.

So I open the never-before-used cabinets,
at least by us,
and wipe them clean,
before neatly arranging
all the dried goods inside,
labels facing forward.

Afterward,
I carefully unpack my weekend bag,
gather all our dirty clothes,
and reset our toiletries in the bathroom.
I wipe down all the surfaces
and mirrors
and begin to work on the last bit
of folding Mom has
from the weekend.

As I do this, Haley and Josh
are off in their own worlds,
flipping through channels,
their indifference infuriating to me,
an indifference I don't understand
or respect.
I want them to get up and do something,
anything,
to make this tension less tense,
but I know that they won't,
that they don't care.

When Mom still isn't back,
Haley makes a sandwich and
Josh fixes a bowl of ramen noodles.

What's Mom going to think?
I say to Josh as I wave my hand at the food.

Josh swallows a bite of noodles slowly
and locks eyes with mine.

Listen, Lieutenant, insulted or not,
we do, in fact,
need this food.
You can waste your time
worrying about her feelings by yourself.
You can starve, too,
he says to me.

You don't even care,
I say to him,
And you care too much,
he says back.

I roll my eyes and get back to work.
I'm almost done putting away
the last of the clothes
when Mom comes back.

After using the bathroom,
she beelines to the bed,

curling up close to the window,
her back to us.

Haley, turn that TV down, and Katie, turn off the lights,
she calls out after a few minutes.
While I rush to do as I'm told,
Haley takes her sweet time
finding the remote
and barely turns the TV down.
And I'm going to say this one time
and one time only—
you three better make sure
your father and his wife
understand that we don't need
no damned charity,
she says to us all.

Eagle Talons

Will the school find out we don't live in the district?
Is Mom still mad? Will she say anything this morning?

My brain is doing overtime this morning,
which means my teachers and my schoolwork
will have a lot of competition this morning.

I float through the morning distracted,
teachers snapping me back to reality
when they call on me to take roll or to answer questions.

Before I know it,
I'm in Mr. Nelson's fourth-period science class,
where checking out is typically easy to do.

I don't particularly like science, or Mr. Nelson.
I mean,
he's nice enough and
he tries really hard to be a planner
but often struggles to keep his class
from getting out of control.
He's a stickler for rules
and I wish he'd loosen up a bit,

which is saying a lot coming from me,
because I love rules.

I'm praying for the day he figures it out.

But in the meantime,
while kids are running their mouths full steam ahead,
utterly ignoring
and aggressively derailing
anything Mr. Nelson might have to say,
I am rejoicing that we're not actually doing any work.

I take out the book I started over winter break,
the one I took from Mom's shelves,
A Painted House,
and start to read,
frantically jotting down quotes that sing,
quotes that sting,
quotes like *I looked at her and tried to speak,*
but all I could think about
was how shocked she'd be
if I said what I was thinking,
which makes me think
about Mom and Dad and
just about every other person
in my life

We're supposed to be learning about ecosystems right now.
I'm not particularly interested
but perk up
when I hear Mr. Smith mention
eagle talons
and how they are able to grip their prey
at ten times the force of the human grip and immediately
I think of Mom
and the way she sinks her talons
into us.

And what I hear Mr. Nelson emphasize,
more so than anything else,
is the fact that sometimes,
an eagle will lose its life clinging to that
which it wants most to hold,
long after it's become apparent that letting go
would ensure survival.

For example,
an eagle can be pulled underwater
by a creature hell-bent on escaping
the eagle's hold.

And ultimately,
if the eagle doesn't let go,
the eagle can drown.

At this,
I think back to Mom
and how tightly she clings to us three,
how adamant she is about refusing to let my father,
or anyone else for that matter,
take us.

And though it is noble,
and though I think I am grateful
to have a mother who is determined
to keep us together,
I wonder if,
like the eagle,
my mother might lose her life
clinging to us,
her children,
long after it's become apparent
that letting go
might ensure survival—
which reminds me
I still need to ask her
why we can't move to Dad's.

What's Wrong?

Alana asks in the hallway after class.
You've been quieter than usual since we got back from break,
she says as we make our way to French.

I mumble something about the funeral and just not feeling
    well,
careful not to say too much.

She asks if I want to sleep over this weekend,
but I know that Mom doesn't have gas to waste,
and even though I know Alana's mom would pick me up,
I can't stand the thought of them seeing where we're living
    now.

I avoid eye contact and
instead of telling her the truth,
I lie and say I'm at my dad's this weekend.

She eyes me suspiciously.
I thought that was every other weekend. Weren't you just there?

But sensing my energy,
she nonetheless lets me have it
as we walk to our next class in silence.

I'm grateful she doesn't push it,
I'm grateful she gives me this space
and hope she doesn't take it personally,
because that would be one more wrong thing
to add to a growing list of disasters.

Bridges I Won't Cross

At the end of each school year,
each grade goes on
an end-of-year trip.

Last year,
we were supposed to go
to Washington, DC,
but because of 9/11,
our capital trip was canceled
and we landed in
Savannah.

So this year,
we are going to DC,
and while I've been excited
about the idea
of getting on a plane
with my classmates
and going all the way to DC,
while I've gotten even more excited
thinking about all the
historical places we will tour,
a pit in my stomach

appears and grows
when everyone talks
about how exciting it will be
to stay in a hotel.

I am torn,
wondering if it's possible
to be excited to leave
one hotel
for another,
not to mention trying
to figure out who I will room with,
since Maia and I aren't speaking.

But let's be real,
that's a bridge
I might not even cross because
I'm not even sure
I'll make this trip.

It's still only January,
but payments are due
in installments,
and I don't see us
figuring this out
anytime too soon,

when keeping up
with the weekly hotel bill
already feels like it's going
to be a hassle,
even with the alternating help of
Ms. Lucille and Dad's weekly child support money,
which leaves so little left over for food and gas.

Sounds Like You

At the end of the day,
Ms. Tyson,
an OG teacher in the very best
and very worst of ways,
returns my drama assignment,
the one I had weeks to finish,
the one I did in a night.
She's drawn brackets next to the missing vocabulary words
and added check marks sporadically throughout.
Her pristine handwriting is roses next to that which she
    approves of
and thorns next to the snarky comments she reflects back at
    me,
wild, enthusiastic comments like
Sound like anyone you know? and
This sounds like you, too!
where I've noted that Helen Keller often sounds like a bratty
    control freak.
Whatever, Ms. Tyson,
I think to myself.

I skipped all the vocabulary
and you still gave me an A, so the joke,
I'd say,
is on you.

Big Breaks and New Beginnings

After school,
I hold the flyer about DC
in my hand,
anxious
to share it with Mom.
Do I show it to her?
When do I show it to her?
But any plans to talk about DC
are quickly dashed when Mom announces
she's applied for a job,
a big job, at that,
in Chicago.

Another midyear, out-of-state move?
I think,
but on the ride home,
I mean back to the hotel,
Mom talks up the potential new job so much
that I'm already thinking
about the kind of life
we'll be able to have
up north.

Besides,
Dad has family in Joliet,
and Mom's family is in St. Louis.
Perhaps it will be nice
to live so much closer to
extended family.
Perhaps we'll have the chance
to develop
the relationships
we've never really
been able to have with
extended family.

Back at the hotel,
our moods are lighter.
We are filled with hope,
which makes it easier to
get along
and laugh along,
though Haley isn't exactly happy
about the idea of leaving
before she's had the chance
to complete her fifth-grade year.

Over the next week
or so,
Mom endures multiple rounds
of the interview process.
She debriefs us
after school each day
on any updates
any insights
any clues
and after a week
or so,
we are hopeful
the job
is hers.

After all,
she is qualified beyond measure
and capable of anything,
and I'm certain this is the
big break and
big change we need
to leave
this hotel behind,

where we can not only find a new and better beginning,

but also where we can start over and

hopefully get it right this time,

and keep it that way,

which seems to be

the biggest challenge of all.

School Zones

It's Friday morning and I'm sitting in homeroom,
listening to the morning announcements
and updates about DC,
a trip I've still yet to tell Mom about,
when Mr. Nelson hands out a letter from the office
to everyone in the class.

Take this home to your parents, he says.

While most kids stuff the paper in their backpacks
and others ball it up for paper basketball,
I take a moment to scan it and see what it has to say.

I don't make it past the first paragraph
before I let out an audible gasp.
It's a notice reminding families
that it is against the law to have your child
enrolled at a school they are not districted for
and that proof of residence can be requested
at any point during the school year.

Part of me acknowledges
that I've seen these sorts of notices before

and that they are randomly handed out
throughout the school year, but for obvious reasons,
the timing causes a pit in my stomach to grow.

What if they request proof of our address right *now*?
What will we do?
What will we say?

Just last week, I was convinced I saw Ms. Pierson,
a particularly ornery staff member,
following us in her car after school.
She tailed us all the way
to Northside Parkway before turning away.
And while I can't say for sure that she was following us,
knowing her,
I wouldn't be surprised.

Now my brain is racing,
thinking about stories I've seen in the news recently
about parents having to pay lots of money
or even going to jail for sending their students
to schools outside their zone.
I think about Mom and how this is the absolute last thing
she'd need right now,
then immediately about us

and the thought that we might have to transfer to a closer
   school,
which would be Campbell Middle School.

Alana recognizes my panic and
asks what's wrong.

Nothing,
I say to her,
folding the paper and sliding it into the planner
I know I won't open tonight.

Nothing.

Library Passes

The following Monday,
Ms. Lucca wants to know what's wrong
when I march into class,
face and body tense,
walking in a straight line to my desk
and immediately putting my head down.

She stands next to my desk
as she gives directions
to the rest of the class to get started,
offering space but also a gentle pat on the back.

And later in class,
when I ask for a pass to the library,
she says yes and signs off without question,
which gently reminds me why
she is the kind of teacher,
as well as the kind of adult,
I want to be when I'm older,
someone who leans in and back
as needed.

I'm Looking for Stillness

Sameness,
steadfastness.

I'm looking for consistency,
sameness,
unwavering sameness.

I'm looking for the opportunity
to stay in one place
so long
that I can look up
one day
and say—
Wow!
I've been here for how long?
which I'm hoping
we'll find
in Chicago.

And if I can't get that at home,
I know I can at least find that at the library,
where you can find any and everything you're looking for,
where you can be still and quiet, too,

where you find still and quiet, too,

where you can set up shop near the librarian,

who is trained to impose more stillness and more quietness

in the rare event your stillness and quietness

may be interrupted, because

there is an enforcer,

a protector,

while you disappear to faraway places

that allow you to get far away from

here.

Dreams Deferred

Mom tells us she is meeting
with the managing director
for what could be her first
senior vice president role at a public relations company.
I'm so proud of her—
senior vice president??
This is such a big deal, and
though I don't really understand
what that means or
what exactly she will be doing,
it sounds exciting and
promising and
like a great opportunity
to get out of here.

But suddenly,
and seemingly
for no reason
at all,
her final interview,
the one that was supposed to be in Chicago,
is canceled.

And just like that,
our dreams of leaving
this hotel and
our fancy plans to
restart up north
are destroyed.

I'm so sick of this, Haley adds.
She'll find something else, I say to Haley and Josh.
Yeah, but what if she doesn't? Josh says to me specifically.

Josh's question in particular lingers,
perfect timing as Mom comes back upstairs
from an extended smoke break downstairs.

Later that night,
after we're twisted in blankets
and curled up
in bed,
long after Haley and Josh
are sound asleep and I'm
certain Mom thinks
I am too,
I hear Mom crying deep, ugly cries
in the bathroom.
These are the types of cries

she's always reserved for the

very worst of situations,

when things are bad,

like *really* bad,

and she doesn't even have

the words to make it sound like

things could get better.

I pull a pillow closer

to muffle the sounds

and fall asleep

with my own

wet eyes.

Deep, Ugly Cries

Later that night,
when everyone else
is fast asleep,
I startle awake
and stare at the ceiling.

It's silent now but
I can still hear Mom's deep, ugly cries.

They are familiar cries, and
in an attempt to go back to sleep,
I begin the process of remembering
all the times
I have heard and seen
these cries before,
these cries that make it seem
as if everything is over and
all hope is lost.

But I know that can't be true, because
Mom is a survivor, and
I have seen her make ways
out of no ways
before
in memories I hold close.

Are We Broken Too?

Stay here with Josh.
I'll be right back,
my mother says to me.
I am four and
our green Eagle Talon
has just gone soaring off
Northern Avenue and
down into a ditch.

Not long ago,
we were making our way to day care from
talking child support at the courthouse
on Memorial Drive at 285.

Rain was hammering down
from an unrelenting sky and
it still is,
now.

Just a few moments ago,
there was a bee in the car
and Haley was crying

and Mom was trying to
get it out.

Just a few seconds ago,
Mom was turning
away from the wheel
to battle the bee,
and I felt the car skidding
as if floating on
water.

One second ago,
I looked out the window
and all I saw
was wet green grass.

I thought to myself,
We're going to end up the grass
and then
not a millisecond later,
in horror,
We're going to end up below
because the wet green grass was
ending and
time and

space were quickly

dropping off and

into a dark, deep ditch of brown

and then and then and then

we were going

down

       down

              down

and though I clenched my eyes closed,

I knew well enough then

to know that there was

absolutely nothing

we,

let alone I,

could do

about what was happening

because it *was* happening

and it *was* happening to *us*.

We have just landed with a thud and a crash

I am convinced could be heard

around the world.

I open my eyes

and see that the car

is broken—
broken metal,
broken glass, and
Are we broken too?
I think to myself.

I hear and feel
the cruel pelting of rain
and wonder who rolled
the windows down.

Haley's cries
are shrieks now
and Mom is frantic,
desperately touching our arms
and legs
and chests
and faces
in turn
to make sure
that we
aren't dead.

We are all alive
but I am not so sure about Josh

as he sits next to me,
silent
and still
as stone.

All the color
in his face
is gone
and he stares ahead,
refusing to answer
when Mom asks
if he is
okay.

Is he broken too?
I wonder to myself,
not wanting to
speak out loud
what I don't want
to be true.

Up above,
through thick
and twisting vines,
I notice cars and trucks zooming by.

We are next to and below the highway,
and I imagine the people
flying down 285
have no idea
that a family of four
is trapped
below.

Who will come for us?
I think
as Mom pulls herself
through the driver's window,
cutting her body
on the jagged edge
to do so.

Outside in the rain,
she reaches back in
and pulls an inconsolable
Haley out after,
clutching her to her chest
and eyeing the steep incline that leads
back to the street,
determined to make her way up
to flag down help.

Stay here with Josh.
I'll be right back,
my mother says to me.

Please take us all,
I plead back through sobs,
because right now,
I want anything
but to be left
alone.

Oh, Katie—
I can't do that.
I need you to stay here,
she says,
before turning
and attempting
to make her way up
shifting Haley to her back,
who desperately clings
to her body.

And so I watch her dig
her nails into earth,
frantically trying to climb up to the street,

her anguished, snot-nosed tears
further blinding her ability to see
where she is going,
the hill she has to climb
proving much too slippery,
too muddy,
too much of a most disastrous mix
of slosh and slop and slime
that ultimately
sends her and Haley sliding
back
down.

It is then
that I see those deep,
ugly cries,
the ones that make me think
this must really be
the end for all of us,
that this must really be
the end of the line.

But it's not.

My mother refuses for it to be so.

She places Haley back in the car with me,
with little, terrified me,
and says,
Katie, I really need your help now.
Stay here with them,
tasking me with watching both
a two-year-old incapable of being comforted
and a three-year-old who won't speak.

I am desperately hoping that nothing bad
will happen in her absence,
knowing I am wholly unqualified
to do anything or protect anyone,
knowing that once again,
I want anything
but to be left alone,
here.

Have you ever *really, really* not wanted
to be somewhere at a specific point in time
but you are there anyway?

All I knew then was that we were there,
together,
whether we wanted to be or not,
until God saw fit for us to be rescued.

Which, to everyone's relief, we were.

Suddenly,
there is a driver who spots my mom
as he is coming down Northern Avenue,
initially unaware that a green Eagle Talon
has crashed in the ditch below
and taken a light pole with it
(something we didn't even know
until much later).

There is another Good Samaritan,
a cabdriver this time,
with rope and a dispatch radio.

Not long after, there are lights
and a siren and shouts of *Down here!*
and before we know it,
we are pulled out of the car and up to safety.

Moments later, we are strapped in the ambulance,
seemingly already light-years away
from the ditch and the unrelenting rain.

Not long after,
we are at the hospital and I am being instructed

to dip my arm into a dark, blood-colored disinfectant
the doctor swears won't hurt.
I am calling him all sorts of animal names,
You pig! You cow! You horse!
when it does—
a four-year-old's equivalent to curse words.

Dad runs in,
crying a mixture of sad and happy tears—
sad because he thought we were dead,
happy because we are not.

Our teachers are here now with balloons and hugs,
but I am still wondering about Josh.

Where is he?
Is he broken?

There are X-rays and a neck brace
and a busted jaw
that requires resetting
and talk of *He will be all right. He's just shaken up pretty bad.*

And though sure enough,
he is eventually okay,

I'll never forget the time I thought
my brother was broken forever.

To this day,
Mom still avoids that road when we venture
to the east side to visit Grandma.

I am most certain that despite our remembering,
Northern Avenue and that ditch
beside and under 285 at Memorial Drive
hold no memory of us.

But I remember,
especially on nights like these,
and try to remind myself that if God saw fit
for all four of us to survive that crash
and to walk away with minimal injuries,
then surely,
He meant for us to survive this, too.

After all, Mom is a survivor,
and I have seen her make ways
out of no ways before.

Trade-Offs

Before I know it,
it's Friday again and Mom announces
we're headed back to Dad's,
that it'll be better for us
than sitting around the room
staring at each other.

Looks like I wasn't lying to Alana after all.

On the ride back north,
I think about how this is
an appreciated break from the hotel
and yet also a cruel, cruel reminder
that an immediate family member
owns a home with empty, unfurnished bedrooms.

Is it possible to be happy and sad at the same time?
Grateful and frustrated?
Appreciative and angry?

I have a feeling Dad won't be
sending us back with any more food.
I'm certain he got a phone call

that encouraged him to keep his food

in his pantries and

send his charity elsewhere.

And while Haley and Josh and I

find ourselves talking more and more

about what life could be like,

about what life would be like

if we stayed here all the time,

we also have to admit there would be

many, many trade-offs.

Mom is more whimsical,

and though that often comes at the expense of

being measured and consistently prepared,

there's never a dream too lofty for her.

You can tell her you want the moon and the stars,

and not only will she convince you it's possible,

but she'll help you go get it,

like

   when I wanted to run for class president in the fifth grade

   and she stayed up with me all night at Kinko's,

   printing flyers and making posters and helping me

   practice my campaign speech,

   which she's promised to repeat in a few months

   when I start my campaign for eighth-grade president.

Or

when I wanted to apply for a highly sought-after
scholarship to attend a civil rights tour in Alabama
just a few months ago and she helped me
perfect my application essay and wouldn't you know it,
I was accepted.

Dad, on the other hand,
is much more reserved,
much more conservative,
much more by the book,
which requires sacrifice on the front end
but guarantees consistent rewards.
He is frugal and
takes his time and
carefully plans out the future,
like
    the expensive Disney World trip we took as a family
    two summers ago,
    and even though we didn't buy one souvenir,
    and even though all our food was prepacked in his trusted
        cooler,
    I still couldn't believe he pulled that trip off.
Or
    how when we lived in San Francisco,
    he saved up for months to buy us Christmas gifts,
    shipping all of them from Atlanta

and hopping on a plane to surprise us for the holiday,
and we spent the day exploring Pier 39
together,
as a family.

With Chicago out and no other prospects lined up,
we three talk about these things,
about the pros and cons of being with Mom
or being with Dad full-time.

Haley says we wouldn't even have any fun here at Dad's,
that Mom will eventually get back on her feet,
while Josh mentions that at least we'd eat all the time,
both of which leave me feeling even more torn
about where I'd rather be
and what matters most.

Why Are We Even Here?

But I'll tell you what I absolutely hate:
window-shopping.

It's Saturday morning
and instead of Sam's,
today we're at Gwinnett Place Mall.
I *want* to believe that Dad means well but
can't help but seethe at his "lessons" and "morals"
about saving money,
about looking but
never buying.

None of this make sense for me right now.
Window-shopping doesn't do anything for me.
I want new shoes and
new jeans and
new makeup and
various other things that would make me feel better
about there being no more Chicago and apparently
no more hope,
that would make me feel more normal
than the circus freak I currently feel like,

walking the mall with my little brother and my little sister

and my father and his wife who refuse to buy anything.

Why are we even here?

I could be back at the house reading

the new Maya Angelou book I've just cracked open,

at best,

or staring at a wall of my choosing,

at worst—

both of which would be way more fun

than I'm having right now.

Hand in hand with his wife,

Dad re-explains that while he *has* the money,

he doesn't want to spend it,

that he and Ning are *"saving for tomorrow"*

as they smile and make love eyes at each other.

Gross. Gross. Gross.

No, Dad, It's Not

Dad's relationship with Ning
moved very fast.

There was no
  I met this woman
and
  I want you to meet her
and
  What do you think?
and
  I think I like her
and
  What would you think if I asked her to move in?
and
  What would you think if I asked her to marry me?
and
  Will you all help us plan the wedding?
or
  Will you all be in the wedding?

It was more like
  I met this woman

to

I love this woman

to

This woman is moving in

to

I asked this woman to marry me

to

I married this woman

to

This woman is now your stepmom

and

Isn't that great?

No, Dad, it's not.

It's actually really, really not.

There Is a Wall Between Us

between Ning and me,
a wall that exists outside of language.

We are simply different.

She is simple and practical,
and though she and I aren't on the same page,
she and my father seem to be cut from the same cloth.

I Want Out

Later on at his house,
when Ning goes to work,
Dad reminds me
that per the child support order,
we get clothes three times a year,
a *clothing allowance*, they call it,
which he carefully plans for,
like everything else.

He reminds me that it's a blessing,
   I know, Dad
that there are kids without fathers,
   I know, Dad
let alone fathers who commit to consistent
clothing allowances,
who do so with duty and joy.
   I know, Dad
But right now,
right now, I don't care.
Right now, it's not enough.
Right now, I don't trust that what I picked out in August
is still in style in January,

and I don't want to be hauled around the Rich's department
   store
with Haley and Josh,
with my mother *and* my father,
picking out school clothes,
one child at a time,
half of my outfits matching Haley's
because that's the way it's always been.

Right now,
I want to go by myself,
shop for myself.

Right now,
I want more autonomy,
more choice,
and more freedom.

Right now,
I don't see none of the positive stuff
my father is trying to make me believe.

I want out of the sheer insanity that is my father's house and
   the ridiculousness that is living out of a hotel with my
   mom—
NOW.

I'm Telling You, Trade-Offs

Speaking of insanity,
Dad tends to bring home rather unusual things we don't
　　want,
things like beach towels adorned with Disney characters
he finds in the lost and found at the country club where he
　　works.

Yuck.

No matter how many times he runs them through the washer
　　and swears they're clean,
we can't shake the smell of chlorine, and
we can't help but remember the remembering they hold,
of somebody else's body,
of their time spent festering in the lost and found for God
　　knows how long,
at a country club where he works,
where we aren't even allowed to visit.

When I see "new" stacks of towels in his garage,
I can't help but remember that the children of employees
are only allowed one annual visit,
a "special day" when the club is closed to members

and club workers can bring their families
and enjoy the facilities they tediously work to maintain
the other 364 days of the year, 365 in a leap year.

I'm mistaken.

We're also allowed to visit on the Fourth of July,
and on the years my father has us that day,
we do,
sitting outside on a perfectly manicured golf course,
watching fireworks decorate the sky,
sitting outside on a perfectly manicured golf course
that employees like my father work tediously to maintain
the other 363 days of the years, 364 in a leap year—
so technically, that makes two days we're allowed to visit.
  Two years ago,
    when I was in the fifth grade,
    Clara Winston invited me to swim at the club.
    Her family were members, and while I looked forward
    to visiting on a day not designated for children of
        employees,
    Dad was nervous,
    worried the club would take issue with my visit.
    But not wanting to discourage me,
    he encouraged me to enjoy myself.

Shortly after arriving,
I wanted to crawl into my skin and disappear.
For as far as I could see,
I was not only the only Black child there,
but the only Black person there
who was not in a uniform
and working.

At the time,
I also had really long braids
I was excited to have,
though suddenly,
I wished they were gone,
those really long braids
floating behind me in the pool
like tentacles
no one wanted to come near.

Dad's nervousness was a premonition.
The club *did* take issue with my visit,
despite the fact that Clara Winston's family
were members.

Ask Jeeves later revealed that the country club
only recently started accepting Black members

which makes me side-eye Dad's allegiance

to this country club

and these discarded towels

adorned with Disney characters,

towels we would usually want,

but let's be clear—

these are rather unusual towels

from a rather unusual country club

that we, quite frankly, don't want

because they come from a rather unusual club

that doesn't seem to want us.

I'm telling you,

trade-offs,

insane trade-offs.

More Walls

Sunday flies by
and before we know it,
we're back at the hotel,
where new barriers
have developed.

What started as a few days has turned to weeks
with no out on the horizon.

To make matters worse,
I'm beginning to think Mom has taken
to talking to the walls in between
the sulking
and the crying
and the stepping out for cigarette breaks.

I can't tell if she notices or minds, and
I can't tell which I think would be worse.

These days,
she talks to walls and she don't mind.
Perhaps walls are mirrors
and she sees

and hears herself
in a way
she's never really felt seen
or heard.

That's the most sense I can make of it,
the best way I can explain it to myself
so I don't feel so small.

Neediness

Sometimes, I'll come home from school
with exciting news,
exciting news for me, at least,
but my news will quickly
become distorted
into *her* news
and *her* plans
and *her* views
and *her* ways of thinking
and feeling
and being
that always trump whatever
I have going on,
or any one of us,
for that matter.

And though I can tell Haley and Josh
have long grown tired
to the point they don't even bother,
I feel in my heart
she needs someone to listen to

more than I need to be heard.

So when she takes over a conversation,

I let her have it.

I tell myself it must mean something more to her,

must mean a lot to her,

and tell myself

that there are other things for me to cling to,

and that when I need her most,

when I am in crisis,

I am still able to command her attention

because once in a sapphire-blue moon,

Mom doesn't talk to walls,

she talks to me.

But on the most recent day-to-day,

there are no signs

she hears me at all

but rather larger signals

that she is waiting,

rather impatiently so,

for me to finish,

so she can bring the conversation back to herself,

back to a memory,

back to a plan,

back to the sound of her very own voice,
and I tell myself she needs this,
more than I need a mother who listens.

I tell myself she needs to hear herself,
more than I need a mother who listens.

And so I find myself arranging
and rearranging
the pieces of my day
so that each afternoon
when I climb into the truck,
I can present to her a more interesting collection
of myself that will compel
a two-way conversation
that breaks free of the constraints
presented by always needing
to figure out the next step,
to break free of the fog
that is suffocating depression,
but come back to the feeling that
perhaps I am not interesting enough,
perhaps I pale in comparison to the
urgency she is experiencing,
the grief she is experiencing,

to all that she is going through
right now.

Perhaps I simply don't have much to offer her at thirteen.
After all,
I can't change our present circumstances,
though I wish that I could.
I know she values what I represent
and takes pride in my grades,
in the accolades and awards I routinely bring home,
but does she really know me?

Does she really know my days?
The steps I take to and from class?
Does she remember the funny joke
Ms. Lucca told in class last Tuesday?
What I'm learning about in social studies?
The names of my friends?
I don't think so,
but I love her anyway,
and tomorrow,
I will try again anyway,
because I tell myself that if it's a wall she needs,
then a wall I will be,
after everything she's been through,
after everything we've been through,

because her need to talk to walls
might just be more important
than my need for a mother
who listens,
even though
my neediness continues to
knead me
into something I don't want to be
but don't know how not to be,
just yet.

Sure Things

Some of my closet friends, like Zahra,
have parents who have been married forever.
Some of them have lived in the same houses forever,
and from the outside looking in,
seem to have a stability and consistency
I've always only been able to dream of.

And while I don't think their lives are perfect,
(they tell me things that show that everything is not always
      what it seems),
I still can't help but wonder if what they have
is still better than what I have—
and definitely better than what I don't.

I know you're not supposed to compare.
I know everybody's lives and situations are different.

I once heard
that if everyone put their problems in a big pile,
everyone would rush to take back their own
once they saw what everyone else
was dealing with.

I want to think that's true but sometimes,
sometimes I can't be so sure.
Sometimes I'm convinced that I want to trade,
that I need to trade in order to be happy,
otherwise I'm going to lose my mind,
on top of everything else I feel like I've already lost.

I want to know about forever.
I hope one day I'll know about forever,
about sure things that don't go away.

It's Hard to Say I'm Sorry

but even harder when
I can't guarantee
I won't ever need to say
I'm sorry again in the future.

And aside from wishing I had the right words to apologize,
I simply wish I had my best friend right now,
because my world is falling apart
and being in between Mom's and Dad's
shared shenanigans is chaos enough,
and I know she'd help me put it back together,
help me brainstorm more songs
for my growing playlist of sad songs
and find ways to help me laugh through it all,
if we were on speaking terms
right now.

Purpose

There's no time to think about sorrys or
crashes or windows or walls
or piles of problems
in Ms. Wofford's class.

After all,
she is a serious planner,
drawing thick lines
in the sand and daring anyone
to cross them,
or her,
which we don't,
because she's strict
and each minute of her
third-period Challenge Language Arts class
has purpose.

Busywork has no place
in her classroom, and neither
does inertia
or chatter
or extended bathroom breaks,

and while she's a thorn
in our sides, a fierce arbiter of
academic precision,
of academic excellence,
I absolutely love her
because on my very best
and very worst days,
she expects me to produce.

A high mark in her class
is worn with pride,
like a hard-earned
battle victory, and I make sure
to show Mom my graded assignments
from her class.

Ms. Wofford pushes me and
says things like,
You're recycling old book reports,
try again
and
Punctuation at the ends
of some lines will help
with readability
and
Try to work on these lines

to keep up with your apparent
rhyme scheme.

Her sparse check marks
affirm my soul, and her
red underlines send
adrenaline through my blood.

Today,
she tasks us with writing
from the perspective
of an inanimate object,
pondering its purpose.

And though I respect Ms. Wofford,
the thought of projecting
myself into an inanimate object
and finding more purpose there
than I feel in myself right now
seems silly and honestly
a waste of time,
a brutal reminder
of the slow hours
I spend in a hotel room with a family
that prefers silence,
these days.

No Sign of Ms. Pierson

or follow-up from that ominous homeroom flyer.

I am less on edge than I was

but still on the lookout for clues,

just in case

our address is questioned.

Perhaps it was only meant to spook,

or warn of some line to be crossed in the future,

in which case,

mission accomplished.

What Purpose?

Back at the hotel,
I start and aim to finish
Ms. Wofford's work first.
But as my pen tap-dances
on a piece of notebook paper,
I'm stuck.

I move from the desk to the window
and see naked trees and wonder
what happens after leaves
crumble and fall apart—
which makes me feel like I'm
crumbling and falling apart—
and what happens
when they've completely disintegrated?
Where do they go?

But enough of leaves.
I don't think
it's supposed to be this way—
this family, I mean.

I've read plenty of stories about families who struggle,
who in the end come together and find hope in each other,
who find love with each other,
when there isn't much else to rely on.
But this isn't one of those stories,
and I don't see us any of us making the kind of
long-term character changes you read about in books
or see in movies
where everyone learns to love each other
where everyone is able to laugh and joke with each other
even if there's no food,
even if we're at the point now where
we're scrambling for change
for the vending machine,
for strawberry Pop-Tarts
and Ritz Bits
and calling it dinner,
or some nights,
coming up with nothing
and sharing nothing
and calling that dinner too,
while Mom looks on,
or not at all,
looking past us
at the walls.

Rainy Dayz

The room is still shrinking,
and I'm more and more convinced
that eventually,
the walls will completely
close in.

Haley, Josh, and I
snap and
rip and
roar at each other
over the desk,
over the phone,
over the computer,
over whose turn it is to hide out in the bathroom.
And while we've never been
anyone's picture-perfect image of sibling love,
if such a thing even exists,
we're monstrous now.

Haley especially hurls insults,
that I'm a suck-up and a show-off,
her sharpshooting skills
insisting I need thicker skin

and maybe I do,

but her daggers are sharp and scathing,

and though her reads may be accurate,

about the ways in which I pine for favor

and accept it at the expense of her and Josh,

her delivery pokes at the wounds that hurt you most,

opening sores and sticking her fingers in,

twisting them around while you

writhe in pain.

Josh's neutrality is noble and infuriating.

Whether he says anything or not,

it is clear he is both judge and jury,

silently taking it all in,

his dissatisfaction and disappointment

clear on his face.

Sometimes,

I just want him to pick a side,

any side,

to reveal where he stands in moments of conflict,

to be the tiebreaker,

but instead,

he often excludes himself.

Whether it's out of protest or disinterest,

I don't know,

though I sense he's solemnly reading us all

and deciding he wants no part

in the chaos he sees.

Lucky him, I think to myself.

Wouldn't we all like to not really be here,

despite the fact that we are all here,

together,

whether we like it or not.

This is a far cry

   from the days when

   Haley and Josh used Mom's digital camera

   to write, record, and edit what they called the Clown

      Mafia Series,

   which featured them taking turns wearing an old

      Halloween clown wig

   and riding around on Josh's skateboard in our apartment

      complex two moves ago,

   their scenes including high stakes and assassinations

   that were so bad,

   they were actually good.

A farther cry from the days

   we spent tooling around Bay Farm Island

   together on our bikes during school breaks,

circling the neighborhood and around the Landing,

a collection of shops and restaurants.

Back then, Mom gave us twenty dollars and instructions to
    stay together

and not do anything foolish

while she was busy working across the bridge in San
    Francisco.

The first part was no problem,

but the second was a much harder task to manage,

considering how often we locked ourselves out of our house

and needed the help of local police

to get in through second-story windows.

An even farther cry

from the times Mom had to use a timer to ensure

each one of us got our turn with the latest Harry Potter
    book,

each one of us getting a two-hour block before having to
    turn it over

with sharp warnings not to spoil it for the next.

The farthest cry

from the days we spent riding bikes and

climbing trees and

exploring old barns that

smelled of oil and sawdust,

back when Dad lived on Mr. Lawrence's farm for three
    years.

Those were the days we were happiest,
the days before we confirmed
that Haley had a different father,
the days before a boulder was wedged between us
and Haley started to question who she could trust,
if anyone at all.

In between the monstrous ripping and roaring,
I think of better days
and desperately hope they'll soon return,
days when we weren't as monstrous as we are now,
even though we've never been
anyone's picture-perfect image of sibling love,
if such a thing even exists.

Fighting Chances

When our claws are away,
there's silence
and stillness,
but not the kind I want,
not the kind I wished for before.

It's a heavy silence,
thick with exhaustion
and surrender
because
there isn't really much to say
because
there isn't really much to do
but wait
for something,
anything,
to come through.

I am lonelier than usual,
even though I can see three other people
at all times.
I try to imagine what they are thinking about
but come up empty

as the room,

inevitably,

continues to shrink.

At this point,

I prefer claws to silence.

Some proof of life,

a smoke signal

of sorts,

that we still

have a fighting

chance,

even though silence feels safe,

because there's nothing

to confront.

Impossible

I'm not a mind reader
but I strive to be one
when Mom won't share what's on her mind,
when she closes off and refuses
to put words to the obvious,
which is that she's
depressed.

I'm not a mind reader
but I strive to be one,
I strive to find the words
to capture the fact that I feel
utterly hopeless to help,
as well as
utterly hopeless to speak up
and change anything.

These are the times I swap
Songs in A Minor
for *Stripped*
and toggle back and forth
between Christina's "Impossible" and
"The Voice Within,"

frantically copying lyrics down in my journal,

double and sometimes triple underlining

lines that speak to me most,

lines that speak for me most,

when I can't speak for myself.

Daydreams

School cafeterias
can be theme parks
or dungeons,
depending on the day.

There are girls who take sides,
some who sidle up closer to me
and others who cackle louder than usual with Maia
since we are not talking,
almost as if this is finally their chance,
almost as if our disunion finally produces
the makings of their very own best friendships
with either one of us.

On these days,
when the courting proves
especially obnoxious,
I take my lunch
and retreat to the library.

The library is a safe space,
a safe space for stillness
and silence

a safe space to daydream
and remember,
to recite and pore over the past,
like how

the week before Christmas break,
Maia and I made a plan
to talk to James
after school.

I told him
to meet me
in the staircase.

We stood on the landing,
Maia a half staircase above
and out of view
so he couldn't see her
but so I could know
that she was there,
for moral support,
so I could remember how I said I felt,
so I could remember what I said I'd do.

I was nervous to confront him,
to share what she told me about him talking to other girls,

to share what I knew to be true,
afraid of his reaction,
which means
I took a while
to get to the point.

And, as if right on cue,
when I eventually said
what I came to say,
what I needed to say,
his face dropped.

First,
he chuckled,
then,
he shook his head in confusion,
and *then*,
as if right on cue,
he started in
on a list of explanations and excuses,
excuses and explanations
that eventually . . .
started to make sense.

I could feel myself being swayed,
wanting to believe him,

wanting to believe him *and*

Maia at the same time,

wanting both of their truths to be possible.

After all,

he was my boyfriend,

but she was my best friend.

I was mortified

because I was slowly starting to feel myself

wanting to believe him more,

and I knew she could sense it,

and I was almost to the point

where I was ready to walk hand in hand

with him out of that staircase

until he said things like

Can you hear yourself?

and

You're being dramatic

and

Who put you up to this? Your friends?

and *that* was when the record scratched.

I let out a chuckle of my own and said,

You know what, this isn't working

and

You know what, I'm good
and
You know what, I have to go

before calling out for Maia myself—
who was still a half staircase above
and out of view,
for moral support,
so I could know
that she was there,
for moral support,
so I could remember how I said I felt,
so I could remember what I said I'd do—
who, right on cue,
stepped down,
leaving James standing
with his mouth wide open,
as she and I
walked hand in hand
out of that staircase.

But That's Not How It Went

That's not how it went,
at all.

Instead,
I believed James,
walking out hand in hand
and leaving Maia
in that staircase
alone.

And though she was initially willing
to talk about it,
my defensiveness and clear desire
to make her see things *my* way
manifested a wall
so tall
and so wide
that it made sense
why our eyes haven't since met,
not once,
in Ms. Lucca's class,
or anywhere else,
in school.

I know now what it says of me,
of what I chose to save
and what I allowed to be lost,
and worry it's too late
to fix it.

The library is a safe space,
a safe space for stillness
and silence,
a safe space to daydream
about what you *wish* you would have done,
to remember what you *actually* did,
to recite and pore over the past,
like how you abandoned
your best friend,
who did everything
not to abandon
you.

All Things Considered

On the way to school these days,
we listen to NPR.
And on the way home from school,
we listen to NPR too—
more specifically,
All Things Considered.

We hate this,
the daily monotone rattling
of world events and retellings
of who's blown up who now
and what piece of obscure legislation
is being thwarted in Congress now.

We hate this,
and would rather listen to Hot 97.5
or KISS 104.1,
but we know better
than to demand control of the radio,
these days.

Today, we climb into the car,
books half falling out

of half-zipped backpacks,
ready to rattle on about our days
and ask what's for dinner.

But because *All Things Considered*
is turned up high,
Mama is quiet,
eyes stone set on the road,
and we know
to be quiet, too.

Running Starts

Back at the hotel each night,
we resume our routines,
rotating between
the desk
and the phone
and the TV
and the bathroom.
Mom's light fades,
and though she's always been little,
she's littler now.

I hug her tight,
in hopes it will stop her from disappearing,
but her deep blues don't grab me back.

I think back to better times and remember that Mom
has always been a dreamer.
With her,
anything has always been possible.
She's a hot-air balloon
in the sky—
whimsical and

vibrant and
capable of great heights.

With her,
you'll see
and know
and come to own
the whole world.

Practical? God, no—
but whatever I've ever even *thought* I could do,
or dreamed of wanting to do,
she's always been there to encourage me,
to cheer me on.

But she runs hot and cold,
especially when she doesn't have any money,
which is every day,
these days.

These days she is particularly frigid and distant,
deflated and grounded and untethered to anything or
    anyone,
least of all us.

These days, we know to steer clear of her,
especially when she is in those quieter-than-quiet moods,
recognizing that we are wholly incapable of fixing *this*,
which right now consists of
zero leads for jobs
and less and less cash
and more and more questions about what's next
and tires that are balding that need replacing.

These days, I make myself smaller than usual,
withdrawing into myself and mirroring her solemnness,
convinced that's the very best I have to offer,
the least imposing version of myself that I can be.

These days, I busy myself with
clearing and wiping
and tidying and cleaning
and washing and folding
and stacking and shuffling
and reading and writing
something,
anything I can think of
to be out of the way and pleasing,
convinced when Mom is ready
to reinflate and take flight again,

that she will be most proud of how I have managed myself,

this space,

this laundry,

my grades,

in her absence,

perhaps in a way that'll convince her

to stay longer next time,

emotionally, at least.

Because she's always here,

physically, at least,

even if mentally and emotionally,

she's far, far away.

But on nights like tonight,

when her blues are deeper than usual

because the Italian restaurant down the street had the nerve

    to deny her a job,

because *even* the Italian restaurant down the street had the

    nerve to deny her a job,

citing her "overqualification,"

on nights like tonight when she sits quietly at the window

with wet, swollen red eyes,

her hands thumbing a near-empty pack of Benson & Hedges,

I know she's far, far away from here

and that no amount of do-gooding will bring her back
    tonight.

And so I grab a pillow and a blanket and curl up on the very
    edge of the bed,
making sure I leave enough space for her and Haley.
I take one last glance at her before I close my eyes,
imagining the extra-strong running start I'll need
to take off flying tonight
in my dreams.

I'm in the Sky Again

but find myself in an empty, bright white space,
which sometimes happens
when I've flown too high,
when I've flown too far away
from everything
and everyone.

I am surrounded by nobody and nothingness,
floating aimlessly in a great nothingness
that somehow
is scarier than darkness.

I know that I have to go back down
and face that which I've been
consistently running from—
though I have no interest
tonight, or any night,
in battling shape-shifting demons,
even if those shape-shifting demons
are me—
because,
quite frankly,
it is terrifying here.

Again

In Ms. Lucca's class,
I stare out the window as rain drizzles,
collecting stalled water droplets and
forming large pools at the base,
which reflects how I feel right now—
sadness collecting more sadness and
making huge balls of sadness
that make me feel like I'm drowning,
that make me feel as out of control
as I did in that crash,
and as powerless to do anything about it too.

Instead of working,
I take out my notebook and write that

Staying in this hotel,
I'm finding,
is a lot like eating ramen noodles.
It's only good
when it's a choice,
and even then,
it's not the best.

But staying in this hotel
for days
and weeks
on end,
with absolutely
no end
in sight,
is downright excruciating.

Again? *you ask in anguish,*
to the room,
to the noodles.
Again! *a monotonous reply*
from the room,
from the noodles.

Again? *I say to the still-shrinking room,*
each morning.
Again! *the room replies.*
Again?? *I say to the high-blood-pressure-inducing*
pack of ramen seasoning,
each time I rip it open
and dump it over a bowl
of steaming noodles.
Again! Again! Again!

When will it be over?

I want to scream
but I'm not sure
if anyone
would hear me
or care.

School Dayz

School continues to be a blur these days,
with me increasingly retreating into a shell
I have no plan of coming out of.

Alana has all but stopped asking what's wrong,
which means I no longer have to fiddle with excuses,
though I want nothing more than to tell her everything.

Meanwhile,
James seems less and less interested in hearing my
    frustrations and sorrows.
Though we still hug in the hallway,
I see him chopping it up more and more with other girls,
who look much more cheerful than me.

I feel I am a dark cloud, brewing with a storm
I soon won't be able to control.

What's for Dinner?

Mom's eyes briefly lock with mine,
before she returns to click-clacking away at her keyboard.

It's the beginning of the week,
which means
we're still a few days shy of Dad's child support,
which means
because we're out of noodles and loose change,
we're out of luck.

Nonexistent meals don't upset me as much as
nonexistent plans,
explanations,
or apologies.

It's the sheer nerve of the look,
almost like I should have known better than to ask,
almost like I should have known better than to be hungry,
let alone bold enough to vocalize said hunger,
when I know perfectly well
that she doesn't have any money.

Are you serious right now?
I think to myself,
at least I *think* I am thinking to myself,
though I am horrified to find that
what I *think* are my thoughts
are actually real words
coming out of my mouth.

Excuse me? What did you say? Mom says,
relocking her now-squinting eyes with mine,
her typing fingers paused in midair.

Josh puts his game down and looks up,
eyebrows raised
as if he's set his attention
on a tantalizing flame growing in size
in front of him.

I said, are you serious?
You won't take food from Dad but you also can't figure out
how to keep food in this room,
and when we point out the fact that there's nothing here,
you have nothing to say?

At this point,
Haley chuckles in disbelief,

sitting up in the bed,

like her favorite movie,

a movie she hasn't seen in a very long time,

is about to begin.

I am outside my body at this point,

pushed out by a racing heart

and stinging tears

that cause my voice to crack

and shake

and tremble.

I am louder than usual,

and speaking more than usual,

but figure that if I'm already

set to go flying through a wall,

then there's absolutely no point

in stopping now.

So with all the boldness I can muster,

I cut the air by scream-crying,

I'm sick of this! I wish we lived with Dad!

Just like that,

the neat boxing

and compartmentalizing

I've tried my best to do
burst at the seams,
and everything falls apart.

Before Mom can open her mouth to reply,
I spin around and
before I know it,
I'm out the door
and down the hall
and in front of the elevator,
jamming the down button with my thumb,
half expecting to hear footsteps and cursing
behind me, but so far,
nothing.

And because the elevator is taking
much too, much too long to come,
I decide to take the stairs
two at a time,
all the way to the first floor from the third,
wiping snot and hot tears from my face
the whole way down,
letting out at the stupid lobby
and pushing through the stupid front doors
to this stupid Extended Stay

and plopping down on the stupid concrete curb,
waiting for
nothing.

I already feel bad
and feel stupid for feeling bad,
but I can't help but imagine
how Mom feels right now.

I know she has to be sad,
I know she has to feel terrible
that she doesn't have the resources
she needs to provide for us,
let alone for herself,
but remind myself that I am
also sad
and feeling terrible
and that right now,
I don't care about her sadness
or anything else,
especially when we ask about dinner
and she has nothing to say.

Right now,
there is nothing more
I want to be able to do right now

than develop the ability

to fly away from this nonsense.

As I get up to see if the running starts of my dreams

hold any weight in the real world, I hear—

He Wouldn't Give You Back,

Mom says as she joins me on the curb.
I don't say anything in response,
and so she continues,
recounting the familiar tale of a messy divorce
but sharing how Dad took us once before,
back when we were small and she announced
that she was leaving.

She tells of how he packed us up and
made the eleven-hour drive to Joliet while she
sat powerless and terrified and sick in Atlanta,
desperately trying to figure out
how to get her children back.

They're his children too,
a lawyer told her,
and according to the law,
he's done nothing wrong.

She tells of how it took her moving to Joliet
and convincing him to come back to Georgia,
how she had to make believe that everything was okay,

just to get him back to Georgia,
just so she could file for divorce.

She tells of how she believes in her heart
that the food he wants to send is a message
that he can take better care of us than her,
that he is more worthy of having us
than her.

She goes back further and tells her own stories
of being split up and dropped off
when she was younger,
Just for a little while,
she was told,
but the days turned to weeks
and the weeks turned to months
and the months turned to years
and she just wanted to be back
with her mother.

She says that even on the worst of days,
when there's no roof of our own,
and no food to be found,
she prides herself
in knowing that at least
we are together,

that she fights
to keep us together,
that we will always
be together,
that she is trying
but knows that she needs
to try harder
to be kinder
in the in-between time
when she's trying to figure it all out,
that she needs help
to figure out her blues
but that she will try harder
to make sure we still feel
that she's there.

I am crying now and so is she.
I turn to hug her and this time,
she hugs me back,
and though it doesn't change everything
or make everything magically better,
it's a start,
because for once,
my mother isn't talking to walls,
she's talking to me.

I Wouldn't Give You Back

Is it true?
  Is what true?
If Mom let us stay with you, you wouldn't give us back?
  What?
You wouldn't give us back?
  Katie.
You wouldn't give us back?
  No.
You really wouldn't give us back?
  No, I wouldn't.
Why?

I am using the phone in the hotel's business center
while Mom stands outside, smoking.

Dad tells the same story Mom just told me,
the one with the spontaneous eleven-hour drive,
but adds details that Mom didn't have,
like how he overheard her late one night on the phone
with plans of her own to leave an unhappy marriage
where they seemed to constantly be at odds,
and like how halfway through the drive
he was nodding in and out of sleep

and unknowingly dozed off,

waking up to himself

veering in and out of highway lanes

with us sleeping soundly in the back.

How he pulled over and sobbed,

sick at the thought that his life was falling apart,

sobbing until he was of the mind

that a few hours of sleep

on the side of the highway

would be best before continuing

the eleven-hour drive north.

How he wanted to believe

that Mom still loved him and forgave him

because he had loved and forgiven her,

but deep in his heart,

knew that she couldn't,

not after what he'd done,

not after he'd taken us and run.

And so against the advice of his family,

who warned him she'd divorce him when they got back to
    Georgia,

he brought us back to Georgia,

and sure enough,

Mom divorced him.

That it took a long time for her to trust us with him again,
that at first,
she'd only let one of us go with him at a time
until she was certain he wouldn't take off with us again,
that he understood because
he wasn't so sure either.

That over the years,
as she succeeded and struggled,
struggled and succeeded,
she scoffed at every extra attempt for help,
which included us living with him full-time,
because he knew she didn't trust that he wouldn't take us
    again,
and keep us this time,
and that she was right,
because now he could afford a better life,
and a house, too,
a more stable life
with consistency and structure.

He speaks of the stillness,
sameness,
unwavering sameness
I believe I want,
I claim to want,

the opportunity to stay in one place
so long that I can look up
one day
and say wow—
I've been here for how long?

But hearing all of *this*,
taking in all of *this*
from Mom and Dad both,
feeling as if I am standing in between Mom and Dad both,
needing to make a decision about
whose side I am on,
even if only in my mind,
I am totally and completely confused, because
what would it say of me to choose to save one
and allow the other to be lost?

At this point,
I am honestly
exhausted
by them both.

Backbones

Mom is still downstairs when I get back to the room.

Haley and Josh poke and prod for answers,
a play-by-play,
details,
but I don't have any.

Instead, I beeline for the bed,
stretching out,
not caring who has space or not tonight,
leaving my books strewn on the floor tonight,
and not bothering to gather them, tonight.

Would you look at that, Josh calls out to no one in particular.
If it isn't the golden child growing a backbone.

Tonight, Haley calls out after him.
Now let's see if she keeps it.

A Start

It's morning time
and I'm up with the realization
that something different happened last night,
that in my dreams,
after I geared up my usual running start
necessary to sustain my usual flight from danger,
I rather suddenly and unusually was able
to control my direction
for once.

For once,
I was able to
decide which way
I wanted to go.

Now if only
I could learn
to stay grounded and face
that which I don't want to face
more consistently,
without waiting around for an explosion,
I'd say I'd be making real progress.

But this breakthrough in direction,
I'm happy to report,
is most definitely
a start.

Growing Pains

The room still feels
like it's shrinking,
but we're navigating it differently now,
ever since I finally decided to erupt.

Haley and Josh help out more
around the room,
and I'm less inclined to suck my teeth
at how they choose to respond,
if at all,
to the comings and goings
of the room.

After all, they're experiencing this too,
and I am not the boss of how anyone should feel or react,
and none of us are really in control of anything,
which makes me think
that Ms. Tyson might have had a point
about my being a "control freak."
Mom is changing too,
paying more attention to
when and what we eat.

One night,
I even show her the flyer for DC,
to which she promptly asks
why I didn't show her earlier,
that we'd figure it out,
somehow.

After school,
she pushes herself to ask
about how our days were
and tries harder to listen
before responding,
and though she's far from perfect,
it's a start,
a deeply appreciated start
from a mother
desperate to soothe the aches
of midyear moves to
Extended Stay hotels.

Mysterious Ways

Mom gets a call
to the room one day,
a call from an old colleague
who says he might have a tip
for a job,
at the giant corporate Home Depot complex across the
    street,
no less,
which sounds *way* too good
to be true.

We try not to get our hopes up
as we cut through the parking lot
and spend the night at the Kinko's
updating Mom's résumé and
making copies on fancy paper.

Using the password
I once watched an employee enter on the computer,
I log all of us in
on separate computers,
Haley and Josh
busy with online games

while I work nearby revising the ending of

my essay for Ms. Wofford.

I've settled on leaves as the inanimate object I'm writing
    about,

and I'm musing on what lies

on the other side

of cracking and falling apart,

if beauty can be found

through changes,

through different seasons.

When Mom is done,

we cut back through the parking lot

and up to the room with quesadillas from Willy's

and prayers up to God

that something comes through.

We cross our fingers and toes and twist

our tongues in the event that counts too.

There will be several rounds,

just like for the job in Chicago,

the job with the unexpected ending,

and I'm hoping this job,

the one at the giant corporate Home Depot complex across
    the street,

the one we've always been able to see

from the front door of the Extended Stay,

is not a cruel joke from God, but

another part of me thinks

that if ever there was a time

to believe again in the notion

that God works in mysterious ways,

that this would be the time.

No News Is Good News

Days pass with no news.
Mom reassures us that no news is good news—
until it's not—
and I want to believe her,
but I'm also not looking forward to the
deep, ugly cries I know very well
may come again in the event
this doesn't work out.

I'm getting used to things
just not working out—
despite really, really
wanting them to,
which leads me deeper and deeper
into my brain,
and heart,
and soul,
burying myself in *I Know Why the Caged Bird Sings*,
capturing lines like
Hoping for the best,
prepared for the worst,
and unsurprised by anything

in between
in my journal and believing
that she wrote this book
especially for me.

The Burns on Her Legs

My outburst has given me new perspective
and pushes me to think about things differently,
including how often I refuse to speak up
about how I feel.

And so during what has become a standard weekend at
   Dad's,
I build up the courage to talk about the strangeness I feel
in this home,
with him and Ning,
with Ning,
and
Speaking of strange,
why does she wear pants
in the hot summer sun?

I learn in hushed tones
about burns and scarring
that tell stories of their own,
stories of her earliest years in America,
years and years ago,
stories of captivity and hard labor,

stories of brutality and hopelessness,
but ultimately,
stories of her refusal to give up,
of her refusal *not* to make it
to the other side of hell.

I knew that Ning and my father were cut from
the same cloth,
but this is much more similar than I initially thought possible
and makes me reconsider
how tightly they cling to each other
as well as my annoyances with their extreme thrift,
extreme thrift that has emerged from
extreme moves made to survive
extreme circumstances.

There is still so much more I want to know,
so much more I need to know,
so much more I need to understand
to no longer feel a wall between us,
to no longer feel like a guest in this house,
to make sure that she doesn't just want my dad
but *us*
and *all of us*,
but for now,

this is a start,
and one I'm learning
might require me
to make more steps forward too.

The Fastest of Them All

After another not-so-spectacular day at school
something spectacular happens.
Mom pulls the Mountaineer into the car-pool line
and what starts as a begrudging, routine walk
to the car turns into a sprint when we
notice Mom's hand emphatically waving out of the window
for us to hurry up
her smile beaming through the glass
almost like she got a job
or maybe even *the* job
and
I got the job! she scream-cries
as we pile into the truck.
There are hugs and tears
and cries and cheers.
So, we're moving? Haley calls from the back seat.
Today! my mother exclaims from the driver's seat.

And just like that,
our move to the hotel's record
for being the fastest move in
our history
is bested by

our moving out
six weeks later.

Apparently,
offer letters and first-month specials
can take you far in a day,
and apparently,
the end of the world won't come
if I don't get to choose *where* we go.

I'm beginning to think that
fast moves might not be that bad
after all.

Sometimes Things Fall Together

just as quickly as they fall apart,
I scribble in my journal
as I take a break from stuffing belongings
into bags and loading them
into the truck.

I want to be grateful, but
I am also frustrated
and angry,
though that doesn't feel right.

If things were always eventually going to get better,
and if the time in between Mom getting a job
and us moving was always going to be this quick,
then why did God see fit for it to be this hard?

I'd like to believe that I can feel all these feelings at once
and still be overjoyed
that we are leaving,
that we are getting the new beginning
we've been wanting and needing.

Open My Heart

It's Saturday morning
and the movers aren't here yet
with our storage.

Here in this new bedroom full of *nothing*,
I look out the window,
knowing new jobs
and new apartments
don't solve everything
but realizing that they doesn't have to
because they are a start.
That new mattresses on the floor
are a start,
that space and room to start over
are a start,
that the blessings of biweekly paychecks
are a start,
that opportunities to practice using your voice
are a start,
that opportunities to practice relinquishing control
because you don't have to run it all
to be happy or to feel safe
are a start,

that chances to understand that *my* response
isn't the *only* possible response to have or feel in a given
    situation
are a start.

And though there's a good chance
we'll move again at some point,
though there's a good chance
things will continue to ebb and flow in the future,
the Extended Stay
we'll inevitably still have to pass
each morning to get back to school,
since we only moved to a new complex
down the street,
a reminder of how things fell
and how they can fall again—
I'm of the mind that everything will be okay.

After all,
this is the way it's always been,
and though it's always been
hard to do, we somehow
always figure it out,
together,
knowing we've made
ways out of no ways before—

out of dead fish
and evictions
and ditches, too—
and God still saw fit for us to survive.

Six weeks into the new year and
I'd like to think that things
are looking up,
which reminds me
that I have one last important start
to make.

With a clear plan for Monday morning in mind,
one that refuses to continue being afraid of spilling out and
    over,
that refuses to be afraid of speaking up and out,
one that begins to think that perhaps belonging to yourself
is more important than belonging to someone else,
I take out my journal,
rip out a few clean pages,
and begin to write:
Dear Maia . . .

The In-Between—

when you're in between
where you want to be and where you are,
when you're in between what you previously had
and what you so desperately want to have back,
when you're in between thoughts and feelings
and wonderings
of what's even okay to think and feel,
when you're in between your parents,
always of the mind that you should be on one side or the
   other,
always of the mind that you should be in one place or
   another,
but having to straddle multiple places at once,
always in the messy middle of something,
perhaps currently in the messy middle of the notoriously
   messiest years of adolescence,
trying to figure out if you want to unload your mess on your
   friends whose lives aren't as messy as yours—

What do you do?
What can you even do?
How do you shift your perspective and
figure out how to be okay

when you're in a supremely chaotic in-between space,

when you're in a supremely slow-moving in-between space,

and there's nothing you can particularly do to speed up time

and be on the other side.

What do you do?

What can you even do?

How do you shift your perspective and

figure out how to be okay

when you don't have a lot of control,

when you can't make many decisions for yourself

or decide on anything, really,

let alone where you live

or how?

What do you do?

What can you even do?

How do you shift your perspective and

figure out how to be okay

when you're no longer a child but

barely a teen,

let alone an adult,

and you're in this messy in-between space

that you just want to get the hell out of,

that you just want to fly the hell out of,

where you can find a place

where the rules are of your own making,

but

you're here now

like the red dots on mall directories,

even though you want

more than anything

not to be—

not to be here with your family,

not to be here in this current situation,

looking in the mirror and sometimes not wanting to even be
    in your skin.

Sometimes the answers are hard

and include things

you *should* do but can't, yet,

while other answers are harder

and reflect things you *would* do, if you could,

things you have no control over,

yet and still,

which can leave you with absolutely nothing to do

but sit around

and wait

in the messy,

boring

in-between.

I've found it's okay not to have all the answers,

that as long as I can learn to let go a little

of how I *believe* things should be,

of how I *believe* people should behave and react,

and own what I can,

which is myself

and an appreciation for what I *do* have,

that everything can be okay,

even if everything around me

is not.

I've found

that the in-between doesn't have to be

the very end of the world and

that sometimes,

we just have to keep going

and face what scares us,

including ourselves,

especially ourselves,

because

sometimes,

that's all you can do.

I've found that all things eventually fall apart,

in time,

even me,

especially me,

no matter how well packed—

and that's okay,

because it leaves space

for better things

to come together.

She comprehended

the perversity of life,

that in the struggle

lies the joy.

I copy Maya's words into my journal and close it,

as I hear the movers arrive

with the first of the boxes.

Figures 1 and 2. Christmas morning 1999: Bay Farm Island, California. In the top photo: Haley and me. In the bottom photo: Josh. Courtesy of Goldie Taylor.

Figure 3. 1997/1998: Atlanta, Georgia. Pictured are some of the artwork and furniture we lost in our move to Florida. From left to right: Haley, Josh, and me. Courtesy of Goldie Taylor.

Figure 4. 2002: At Dad's apartment off Sidney Marcus Boulevard, before he and Ning moved to their house in the suburbs.
From left to right: Me, Josh, Haley, and Ning. Courtesy of Edward Van Heidrich.

Figure 5. 2000: At my grandmother's home on Fieldgreen Drive.
Pictured left to right: me, my great-aunt Gerald (rest in peace), my grandma, my grandma's late dog Maggie, and my mom. Courtesy of Joshua Van Heidrich.

Figure 6. Summer 2001: Disney World. Pictured from left to right: Josh, Haley, and me. Courtesy of Edward Van Heidrich.

Figure 7. 1997 or 1998: Six Flags with
Dad. Pictured left to right: me, Josh, and
Haley. Courtesy of Edward Van Heidrich.

Figure 8. The guest room at Dad's (the Monopoly game sits on top of the shelf, with the brown pullout couch at the bottom right). Pictured left to right: Josh, me, Dad, and Haley. Courtesy of Wilai Van Heidrich.

Figure 9. 2000: After we moved back to Atlanta from California. Left to right: Dad and Mom. Courtesy of Katherine Van Heidrich.

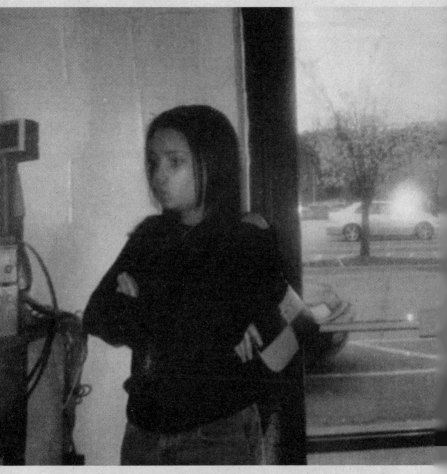

Figure 10. 2003/2004: Me, miserable at Sam's Club, per usual. Courtesy of Joshua Van Heidrich.

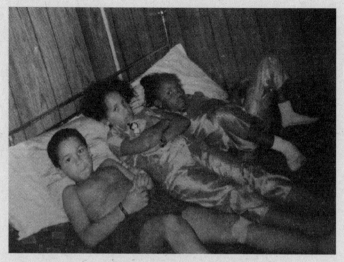

Figure 11. Circa 1998: A typical weekend at Dad's, in pajamas. Pictured left to right: Josh, me, and Haley. Courtesy of Edward Van Heidrich.

Figure 12. 1999: Boca Raton, Florida, me playing "school." Not pictured: Haley and Josh forced to be my "students." Courtesy of Goldie Taylor.

Acknowledgments

Thanks be to God for all the ways in which He continues to endow me with strength I didn't know I had, grace I know I don't deserve, and love that is uncompromising and steadfast.

To my children, Brandon and Nasir. Being your mom is my greatest honor and accomplishment. I'm in constant awe of your creativity, thoughtfulness, and humor and couldn't imagine this world without the two of you in it or your little voices assuring me I am a "good mommy."

To my family. To Mom, thank you for always believing in my dreams and encouraging me to write the stories I needed to, without regard for anyone, even if that meant you. I am so proud to be your daughter and am continuously learning from you how to bet big on myself. Thank you for getting us out of that ditch on Northern Avenue, and for getting us out of countless ditches since then. To Dad, thank you for being my biggest cheerleader, for your silliness and your life lessons, for hearing me and adjusting, for always showing up for me and my family, for cheese grits and freeze pops. To Ning, thank you for taking care of Dad, for loving him and us, for being an amazing Amma to my boys, and for panang curry ribs that fall off the bone. To Josh, thank you for breaking down my boxes, making me tacos, and telling me when I draw my eyebrows on too thick. You are forever my wonder twin. To Haley, you once told me, "We have babies who need us to be happy." May we both be able to achieve a level of peace and joy that sustains us and transcends the past. To Taylor, you are brilliant, curious, and kind and the absolute best big cousin to Brandon and Nasir. You will always be our Violet. To Grandma, thank you for all the inspirational quotes, books, art, and crafts you send me. They hold me up and help me always feel close to you.

To my school community, thank you for encouraging me and hyping this journey, for giving me space to be myself as I do the work I love with students. To my 2013–2014 fifth graders, A. C. and J. S., thank you for all the grace you extended to me during my first year of teaching, for staying close and supporting me as much as I worked to stay close and support you. To my 2017–2018 fifth graders, S. M., A. H., J. K., and A. Z. Thank you for reading my early drafts, helping me track my querying journey on anchor chart paper in the back of my classroom, and for encouraging me on the "power of no" through denials and delays.

To my teachers. To Ms. Spadaccini, I don't say this lightly when I say thank you for saving my life and keeping me whole. You checked on me, encouraged me, pushed me despite me firmly believing I hated math, but most importantly, assured me I'd have more agency to make my life what I needed it to be when I got older. To Madame Simmons, thank you for taking me to every Brown University informational session we could find in the city, for all your super-direct but incredibly heartfelt advice, and for making sure I had grocery money if ever I needed it.

To my friends of mind, the women who gather and carry me when

I have trouble doing it for myself: Ashley Alvarez, Gabby Logan, Brittany Jones, Jasmine Newson, Rianne Elkun, Tracey Battle, and Taylor Pettway. To coworkers turned family, Irma Gonzalez, Leticia Dorado, Kym Scherbarth, and Chellsee Lee. To lifelong friends, where time and space and distance remains nonexistent, Gabrielle Lopez, Tia Ware, Allie Watson, and Angel Ballard.

A very special thank-you to my phenomenal agent at WME, Janine Kamouh. You have been a dream to work with, an ever-positive force who has relentlessly championed my stories. I am so grateful to know you and amazed by how you balance being a powerhouse of an agent and a powerhouse of a mom. To Alyson Heller and the entire Aladdin/Simon & Schuster family: thank you for the passion and energy you've brought to my work, for giving me the opportunity to share my story with the world, for thoughtful and careful edits, for allowing me to go as deep or stay as shallow as my heart needs to.

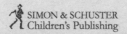